Business plan template and example: how to write a business plan

by Alex Genadinik

ISBN: 1519741782
ISBN-13: 978-1519741783

DEDICATION

Dedicated to my mother and grandmother who are the biggest entrepreneurs I know.

CONTENTS

FOREWORD

I wrote this book with care and compsassion about your business and your journey as an entrepreneur. If you are just starting your business, I understand how difficult it might for you at the moment because I've been where you are now.

The advice in this book is based on the accumulated experience and success of planning, starting and succeeding with my own business, and coaching 1,000+ entrepreneurs just like you who are my clients.

I am the creator of some of the top business planning mobile apps for Android and iPhone. I also teach one of the most popular online business planning courses, and I regularly work with entrepreneurs to help them create a business plan and various strategies for their businesses.

In sharing the knowledge in this book, my hope is to make your journey as an entrepreneur an amazing one. I wish you best of luck and. I hope that the ideas in this book will contribute to your success. Enjoy the book.

Before we start

Hello, I am excited that you got this book. I appreciate you putting your faith in my work, and I want to extend a very warm welcome to you. In writing this book I did my best to cover every element that I think will help you get the most out of your business planning efforts.

While I did my best to cover every element that I thought would help you, there is always more I can do to improve the book. If you feel that the book can benefit from some additional information on some topic, send me an email and let me know. I promise to take your advice seriously, and I'll appreciate that you took the time to write.

And if you love the book and don't see any need to improve it, I'd still love to hear from you at any point of your journey through this book with either questions, comments, or if you just want to introduce yourself and your business.

My personal email address is:
alex.genadinik@gmail.com

I look forward to hearing from you.

i. GIFTS FOR YOU

What you are reading is the 3rd edition of this book. I've been thinking long and hard about how I can help you more each time I re-write the book, and I've come up with a list of free resources beyond this book that you can use to further benefit your business.

At the end of this book you will find 3 additional resources that I made available for you for free as my gift to you just for getting this book.

ii. GET TO KNOW ME AND MY WORK

Business is personal.

At one point I hope to get to know you. And here is how you can get to know me.

Here is a page with a video where I share my journey as an entrepreneur so you can get to know my story:

http://www.problemio.com/about_us.php

Thank you for taking the time to get to know me. One day I hope to get to know you.

iii. ADDITIONAL BOOKS THAT CAN HELP YOU

1) Marketing Plan Template - this is the sister book for this book. Every business should have a strong business plan AND a strong marketing plan. A marketing plan is just a part of your overall business plan.

https://www.amazon.com/Marketing-Plan-Template-Example-marketing-ebook/dp/B0190HXUYG

Shortened URL if you are using a print copy of this book:

https://goo.gl/YU7sw6

2) 10 Fundraising Strategies - almost all entrepreneurs ask about raising money, and you may be wondering about it too. This book gives you 10+ different strategies to raise money for your business.

https://www.amazon.com/10-Fundraising-Ideas-Strategies-strategies-ebook/dp/B00KADT0Q2

Shortened URL if you are using a print copy of this book:

https://goo.gl/3fqmBr

3) 20 Productivity Principles - this book will help you get more done regardless of what you are working on. I put together 20 different fields of productivity, each of which can give you the strategies to align your work in order to get more done starting today and every day for the rest of your life.

https://www.amazon.com/Principles-Productivity-Motivation-Organization-Procrastination-ebook/dp/B06X96T4FZ

Shortened URL if you are using a print copy of this book:

https://goo.gl/m6PZQ1

Here is a full list of my 20+ books on Amazon:

https://www.amazon.com/Alex-Genadinik/e/B00I114WEU

Shortened URL if you are using a print copy of this book:

https://goo.gl/WWBcao

Note: if you are in the UK, change the .com in the URLs to .co.uk

CHAPTER 1: INTRODUCTION TO BUSINESS PLANNING

"Whether you think you can, or you think you can't, you are right."

- Henry Ford

1. What is a business plan

I'll tell you two things that a business plan is, and one thing it isn't.

The first thing that comes to mind for most people when they think of business plans is a formal business plan document that you either hand to some company or investors or keep for internal company use.

The second thing that a business plan is, is a cohesive plan of action for how you will execute every part of your business. This doesn't have to be written on a piece of paper or typed out. You can plan your business strategy in your mind. What is important is that you have a *viable and quality plan of action* before you start your business, and you aren't just plunging into your business blindly. This plan isn't to hand to anyone else. It is meant to help you organize your ideas and have a viable strategy for your business.

Now let me tell you what a business plan isn't. Don't think about it as you would think about a homework assignment like an essay that must be completed or handed in before you can start your business. It also isn't something that you have someone else create for you because you aren't sure how to do it on your own. And it certainly shouldn't be your excuse to procrastinate on the actual work you need to do to start your business.

I like to define the business plan as cohesive strategy for your business that you may plan in your mind or in a written document which explains each major component of your business, how those major components will work well with one another, and your plan for the execution of the business.

If you are not sure how to create an effective business plan and you are a first-time entrepreneur, learning how to plan your business like you are doing with this book is a very good first step. Learning empowers you long-term. You will be able to use what you learn about planning a business for your current business and every new business idea you have in the future. As an entrepreneur, you must make it a habit to always keep learning and improving your skills.

In addition to learning, it might also be helpful for you to get coached on planning your business so that you can learn and get guidance from an experienced business person while you are both working on your business plan together. But don't just pay someone to have it written for you just to feel good that you have it.

Keep in mind, as one of my gifts to you that come along with this book, I am offering to give you feedback on your business idea or your business plan. Of course, since I can't read everyone's full business plan, please wait until you get further in the book and learn how to create the simple 3-sentence business plan. Send that to me for feedback and I'll be happy to hear from you and give you my feedback and suggestions. At the end of the book you can find about all the extra free resources I put together for you.

2. When you need a business plan

Many people write to me and ask whether they need a business plan. My answer is always simple. There are two instances when you should write a business plan. The first situation in which you need a business plan is when some individual or organization that you want to work with specifically asks for your business plan. The other situation when you should have a business plan is for yourself to help you organize your ideas.

As you can probably guess, even if you don't need to write a formal business plan to give to an investor or some organization, you should always go through a rigorous planning process for your own sake to create a good strategy for your business. In my opinion, that is the true value of business planning.

Writing a business plan, even an informal one, can help you organize your ideas and refine your overall business model. The process of thinking about, and planning your business holistically can help you catch and correct many mistakes before you start. It is much more expensive to realize that you are heading in the wrong direction after you have already started your business than during the planning stages. The value of business planning is to find the problems in your initial business idea, and find ways around those problems during the planning stage while it is very cheap to do that.

Make sure you spend enough time planning your business and fixing potential problems in your overall business strategy as early as possible. As a rule of thumb, the later you find problems with your business, the more expensive and more time consuming it will be to fix those problems.

There are many additional benefits to writing the business plan just for yourself. First, you can have a single concrete document in which you and your business partners can agree on the structure, and execution details of the business. Another benefit is that it gives you something concrete where your ideas are laid out. You can use it to facilitate discussions within your team about each aspect of the business, and brainstorm ideas to refine various aspects of the business plan. This process will help you catch many potential pitfalls.

Now let's take a look at what makes a good business plan.

3. What makes a good business plan

What makes a good business plan isn't the formatting, long length, or whether you use fancy big words.

What matters above all else is whether the strategies in your business plan are viable.

If you are a first-time entrepreneur, it might be difficult for you to determine whether the strategies in your business plan are good because this is your first business and everything is new. Even experienced entrepreneurs including myself can make mistakes because all of us have blind spots. Plus, sometimes we simply don't know what we don't know, and no one knows everything. It is human to make mistakes. No one is mistake-free. Once you put aside your ego and make peace with the idea that you might make mistakes and oversights, it will be easier for you to seek the right kind of extra help to make sure that the strategies in your business plan are as good as they can be.

For that reason, if you are a first-time entrepreneur, get someone to coach you on strategy for your business plan and have experienced business people look it over and give you feedback. Someone with experience can often easily spot a blunder that may waste a lot of time and money if they creep into your business strategy.

I am not saying that it should be me, and I certainly don't want to make it seem like I am selling any of my services here. In fact, I made a number of free resources available for you at the end of the book. So please don't think that I am selling anything here. But if you are a first-time entrepreneur, it would be wise to seek mentorship or help from someone more experienced.

When I look back at my own journey as an entrepreneur, some of the big mistakes I made in the past could have been easily preventable if someone could have pointed out those mistakes before I embarked on making them, and pointed me in the right direction.

4. What is a business model?

There are many different ways to look at what is a business model. Most of those are unnecessarily complex. Let me suggest a simple definition that we can use.

Business model definition: how every component of your business works on its own, and in relation to every other component of your business.

Let's unwrap that definition. When you look at a business, it is made up of many different parts. Some of the parts are marketing, creating and improving the product, the finances, the employees, the consumers that are targeted, inventory management like storage and shipping of products, and much more. What is important in a business model is that all of these different aspects of the business should be great individually while also working well with one another. In theory, this might sound simple to accomplish. But in practice, it is extremely difficult to come up with a great business model where everything fits just right. As businesses are started and grown, the management team must constantly refine and improve every component of the business model, and how those components work together.

Neither your business model nor your business plan are static things. They evolve over time and you must constantly work to refine and improve them. The better your business model can be during the planning phases of the business, the better off your business will be from the very beginning, and your business will be better positioned to succeed long-term.

5. My personal journey into business plans

If you are reading this book, most likely you are in the process of starting your first business or you are in the early stages of your journey as an entrepreneur.

First of all, congratulations on starting. I hope you achieve tremendous success and enjoy every day of your journey as an entrepreneur.

At one point I was at the exact same stage of my journey as an entrepreneur as you are now. I understand some of the emotions and experiences you might be going through.

It isn't easy to start your own business. It is confusing, daunting, and stressful in more ways than one. There is financial stress, social stress put on you by friends and family, and then there is the stress from self-doubt, isn't there? Until we are successful, we have no idea when that moment of success will come, whether it will ever come, and how long we will have to struggle before success finally arrives.

When I started my first business, I had no experience or background in business. My education is in Computer Science. Absolutely everything was new and confusing. Everyone else seemed to have an opinion as to what I should do with my business, and most of those opinions seemed pretty good at the time because I had not developed the business sense that comes with experience. And since I had no way to think through ideas or strategies, I just plowed into business ideas and business strategies without too much business planning.

And even if I did do the business planning on my own, what could I really plan? I had no way to tell whether one strategy was going to be better than another. All my plans were going to be of amateur quality at best.

As you can guess, without any planning or experience to fall back on, my initial businesses were disasters that crashed and burned. Ouch! But this is why I wrote this book: precisely so that you get the support and good advice I didn't have, and that you don't make the mistakes I made.

As time passed and I picked up many business skills and experience, I realized that if only I had a mentor to guide or advise me, in just a few minutes of conversation they could have quickly noticed my previous beginner mistakes, pointed them out, prevented me from making many costly errors, and saved me months of effort and a lot of wasted money.

Once I became a more experienced and stronger entrepreneur, I wanted to help other entrepreneurs who were just starting out by giving them the knowledge and tools to avoid making the mistakes I once made.

The first such tools I built were mobile apps that helped people write a business plan.

Those apps were reasonably successful, and at the time of writing this book (even this book's original draft), over 1,000,000 entrepreneurs downloaded those apps across

Android and iPhone. While the apps were helping the entrepreneurs who were using them, I was noticing that the entrepreneurs who were using my apps were still struggling in 6 areas of their businesses:

1) Getting and choosing the right business ideas
2) Raising money
3) Promoting their businesses
4) Business planning
5) Accounting issues
6) Legal issues

I am not an accountant or a lawyer so I decided not to touch the legal or accounting issues, and focused on the 4 remaining major problem areas for entrepreneurs by turning my business plan app into a 4-app business-starting series that completely guides people from through:

1) Business idea stage
2) Business planning
3) Fundraising
4) Marketing and growing a businesses

These apps are all free. If you are curious to take a look at how they work, there is no risk to try them. You can find all my apps on my website:

http://www.problemio.com

If you are wondering why my website is named Problemio.com, it is because it is rooted in the word "problem" which is a play on the old traditional business question of "what problem is your business solving?" which asks for the very initial core fundamental since a business has to provide some benefit to someone.

My experience of seeing and helping so many entrepreneurs on my apps gave me enough insight into what entrepreneurs needed to then go on to create a YouTube channel for entrepreneurs, online business courses, coaching programs, and eventually this book.

Now let's begin learning how to write the business plan.

CHAPTER 2: INTRODUCING THE 3-SENTENCE BUSINESS PLAN TO HELP YOU START WITH THE SIMPLEST POSSIBLE BUSINESS PLAN

"If you can't explain it to a six year old, you don't understand it yourself."

- Albert Einstein

"Life is really simple, but we insist on making it complicated."

- Confucius

1. 3-sentence business plan introduction

At one point in my work of thinking through the strategies for countless companies, it dawned on me that almost all these companies had something in common. All companies had some product or service. All companies needed to promote their products or services. And all companies needed to ultimately reach some kind of financial health in order to be self-sustaining.

These three parts of a business (product, promotion, finances) are the core of any business, and to help my clients be able to get into business planning with less pain and struggle, I came up with the 3-sentence business plan.

The goal of the 3-sentence business plan is to simplify the business planning process to the bones to make it as simple as possible. At its simplest level it will be easy to express and think through the core of the business in as little as a few sentences.

And with that, the simplest entry into business planning was born. Let's take a look at two examples to solidify this concept.

2. 3-sentence business plan example for a tech product

In this section I'll show you how simple a 3-sentence business plan can be. The example we'll use is business plan app. I am using that example for three reasons. The first reason is that because it is a live product, I can use the wisdom of hindsight to give you insight about it as a business. The second reason is that you can actually take a look at that product yourself to understand what we are talking about. That is better than basing an example on some theoretical product that might be difficult to explain and understand. The third reason I am using the mobile app as an example is because I am trying to give you different perspectives on how to write a business plan. In the next section we will take a look at a 3-sentence business plan for a very different business which is a lawn care company.

Here is an example of such a business plan.

Product: mobile app to help you write a business plan.

Marketing: app store search, publicity, social sharing.

Finances: revenue will come from subscriptions and upsells of educational business products and coaching.

The way this app worked out was that because as a software engineer, I was able to build it on my own for free, any revenue was pure profit. The main marketing strategies that worked were app store search, publicity and social sharing with 98% of all downloads coming from those three promotional sources.

Do you see how easy it can be to paint the picture for a whole business with a good outline of the core parts of the business? Now let's take a look at the 3-sentence business plan for a lawn care business to get a very different perspective.

3. 3-sentence business plan example for a lawn care business

Let's take a look at an example of a lawn care business. It is a traditional business that everyone has encountered before. Here is the example:

Product: residential lawn care.

Marketing: YellowPages, Google search, Yelp.com and other local business listing websites, paying for ads, referrals, classifieds, business cards & business networking, fliers.

Finances: We will focus on long-term customer retention to cover customer acquisition costs, pay employees less than we charge customers, and keep the difference.

See how simple it can be to express an almost entire strategy for a business? Now let's try an exercise to help you create your simple 3-sentence business plan that we will later expand into a 1-page business plan and then a full-length business plan.

4. 3-sentence business plan exercise for your business

In this section we'll do an exercise and a fun challenge.

The exercise will be to write your own 3-sentence business plan. Here is a template for you:

(It is ok if you use more sentences than just three. Approximately 3-6 sentences is fine).

Product:

- What is the product or service?

- What benefit does it provide and to whom?
- Can you make it cheaply or of high quality?
- What advantage do you or the founding team bring to it?

Marketing:

- What will be the marketing (free promotion), advertising (paid promotion) or direct sales strategies that are a great fit for the product?

Finances:

- What are the major sources of revenue?
- How will this happen profitably?
- When will you get to financial sustainabiltiy?

Just answer the questions that make sense for your unique situation, and you will have completed your 3-sentence business plan.

Now for the fun challenge that will make this book into more of an interactive experience. Do you want to test how good your 3-sentence business plan is? I can take a look at it and give you my feedback.

Just email me your 3-sentence business plan with the subject "3-sentence business plan" to my personal email address: alex.genadinik@gmail.com

Please write your 3-sentence business plan in the body of the email without any attachments so that it is easier for me to read your business plan. I'll reply with my thoughts on your plan and my honest feedback.

Please keep in mind that I get an overwhelming amount of email every day. I'll do my best to respond as quickly as I can. If you don't hear from me within the first 24 hours, please be patient, but if you don't hear from me within a week, just send a reminder email.

CHAPTER 3: NEXT BABY STEP IN BUSINESS PLAN COMPLEXITY: 1-PAGE BUSINESS PLAN

"Progress lies not in enhancing what is, but in advancing toward what will be."

- Khalil Gibran

1. 1-page business plan introduction

While the 3-sentence business plan was my own invention to help you ease into the process and thinking that goes into business planning, the 1-page business plan is something that you may be asked for by investors or anyone else who wants to briefly familiarize themselves with your business without spending too much time on the details.

In this section we'll expand the 3-sentence business plan into a full 1-page business plan which is something that you can begin showing to different people if they ask to see it.

2. 1-page business plan example for a tech product

Title: Mobile app 1-page business plan

Product:

The product is a series of mobile apps on Android and iOS. The apps will help people create a business plan and aid them in starting a business.

The apps will help people plan their businesses in these 3 ways:

- Tools to help people plan and save their plans right on the app
- Educational tutorials to guide beginners
- Live help on the app

Marketing:

The marketing of these apps will be through mobile app store search, publicity, our website, and social sharing from people inviting business partners to help plan their businesses on the apps.

Since for most apps, the bulk of their downloads comes from app store search, that is where we will concentrate.

Monetization:

We will make money by up selling educational business products, coaching and in-app purchases.

Profitability:

Since the app has minimal costs to build and maintain it, almost all revenue is immediate profit.

Target customer:

Young entrepreneurs, first-time entrepreneurs, people who need help, guidance and tools planning a business.

Size of opportunity:

These apps can reach over 1,000,000 people per year at their full potential.

Founding team:

Alex Genadinik is the founder and the main engineer. This is a single founder business. I'll outsource design work, but can handle all the other tasks.

Previous funding:

None

Costs:

Under $2,000 per year for initial design and ongoing outsourcing.

3. Analysis of a 1-page business plan example with a tech product

With this 1-page business plan for a mobile app we took a baby step and expanded the 3-sentence business plan for a mobile app from the previous chapter into a full 1-page plan.

All it took to go from a 3-sentence business plan to a 1-page business plan is a slight elaboration on the three core components of a business plan, and the addition of secondary sections like team, costs, and previous funding.

There was also the addition of sections that talk about the target customer and the overall size of the opportunity. I left out the competition section, but that may also be added. These sections are important to have in a business plan of this length and longer. Plus, you should never start a business without having a deep understanding of your target customer and your competitive business landscape.

4. 1-page business plan example with a traditional business

Title: Lawn Care Business Plan

NOTE: the statistics noted in this business plan and this business are not real. They are made up for the sake of creating this example.

Executive Summary

Bob's Lawn Care operates within San Francisco, California and services the area within a 30 mile radius of the city.

Product Overview

The company offers residential lawn care, landscaping and yard work. The main focus is on providing affluent residential lawn care services.

Current Progress Of The Business

The company was founded in April 2012. Since then we have opened a small office and hired a salesperson and two full-time employees.

We currently have 25 residential accounts which we service on a monthly basis.

Our current growth is approximately 5 residential accounts per month while losing about one per month.

Target Market

Our focus is the high-end residential market. Our research shows that there are 120,000 single family homes in the area which we service.

Market Size

From industry research, we know that approximately 40% of affluent homes hire lawn care companies to maintain their lawns. That leaves us with a market size of about 45,000 residential homes.

Additionally, there are 1,000,000 non-affluent homes in the area, 5% of which hire lawn care companies, which adds another 50,000 homes.

Additionally, there are 10,000 apartment buildings, 80% of which use lawn care companies.

That brings our total market size to 105,000 residences. The average account size brings in an annual $5,000 per account which makes our total market opportunity: 105,000 residences multiplied by 5000 dollars = $525,000,000 per year.

Competition

We compete with numerous lawn care and landscaping companies such as John's Lawn Care and Pete's Lawn Care. We are different from most of our competition in the quality of work that we provide.

We provide higher quality work at higher prices, which enables us to target more affluent consumers which will lead to higher margins. Due to our higher quality of service, we will also retain customers for longer periods of time.

Financials

Our current annual revenue from our 25 accounts is $125,000 per year. Our major costs are:

1) Staff salaries for the 4 current employees: $120,000.

2) Office space: $20,000 per year.

3) Equipment and vehicles: $30,000 per year.

4) Additional, smaller and 1-time costs: $10,000.

Total costs are $180,000 which brings us to a net loss of $55,000 per year.

Marketing And Sales

We are currently marketing via 3 methods:

1) Direct sales and reaching out to potential clients.

2) Building a professional referral network with other local service providers.

3) Online advertising via our website, search and listings on other local-service websites.

Current Team

Bob, CEO and founder, has over 20 years experience in the lawn care industry and previously ran a successful lawn care company in Los Angeles which he sold when he moved to San Francisco.

The rest of the team is:

One sales person and two people who go to locations and provide the lawn care services.

What We Are Looking For

We are looking for a business loan of $300,000 in order to fund our growth via marketing and sales for the next two years and help us get to 500 accounts which will equal to annual revenue of approximately 2.5 million.

5. Analysis of a 1-page business plan example for a traditional business

You might say that this business plan was a little bit longer than one page and you will be correct. I expanded on our 1-page app business plan in order to take another step up in complexity as we work our way to writing the full business plan.

The only thing I did differently here is I dug a little bit deeper into the financials of this business. I elaborated on the costs, the target customer, the revenue and how this business would become profitable.

Now let's move forward and learn how to write a full business plan. Since we already have the 1-page business plan, this step is not as scary as it would have been if we were starting from nothing.

CHAPTER 4: HOW TO WRITE A BUSINESS PLAN

"If you fail to plan, you plan to fail."

- Benjamin Franklin

The sections below are the sections of a typical business plan.

Each section has:

-   Theoretical tips on how to write that section
-   Practical suggestions on how to approach that part of
    the business strategy for the real world execution of
    your business
-   An example excerpt of that business plan section from

       a full business plan
-    Analysis of that excerpt

This way you get a combination of theoretical and practical advice on how to approach each section of the business plan, have a template to work from, and have an example and its analysis for reference.

In my opinion, the biggest value in this is from the practical advice on how you can approach each of the issues in the real world because that practical aspect during your execution of the business will ultimately be what will make your business successful.

Even if you don't want the practical advice and just want me to show you how to write a business plan, you get a template to work with, and an example and an explanation for how to write each section in the business plan template.

Even if you are not writing a formal business plan, you must think deeply through each of the sections of a business plan before you start your business.

NOTE: Since the business plan is broken up through the sections of this chapter, if you want to see the full business plan in its entirety, you can find it in the appendix section after the last chapter of this book.

My question to you: in the latest edition of this book I started doing something different in every section of this chapter. The addition of an example and analysis from a real business plan in each section of this chapter is something new I added in the latest edition of this book. My question to you is whether you find this helpful, or cumbersome and confusing? I'd love to hear from you about that. My personal email address is:

alex.genadinik@gmail.com

And by the way, if you find this book helpful, I would appreciate it if you can let people know about it by adding a nice review on Amazon because you can bet that the people who might not like the book will surely find something negative to say, and it would be great if people who like the book made their opinions known.

1. Executive summary

The executive summary is a paragraph or two that acts as the introduction to your business plan. This is a general overview of the problem that your business is solving. It can also contain your company's mission statement. Use the executive summary to prepare the reader for the issues you will cover in the rest of your business plan. You should briefly explain what your product is, but do not go into too much detail about the product or other components of your business. You will have a chance to get into details in subsequent sections.

Quick note: some industries have another meaning for the term "executive summary" which is a very shortened business plan that is only about 1-2 pages. Just don't get these confused.

Example of an executive summary from a business plan for my mobile app

I am building a full 4-app mobile app series on Android and iPhone that will help people plan their businesses, and support them all the way through planning, starting and growing their businesses.

This is a revolutionary new take on mobile apps where the apps become the business coach and guide for entrepreneurs, and give entrepreneurs the support they need to succeed.

The reason there are 4 apps in the series is because each app covers one of the biggest challenges for entrepreneurs:

- *Business idea stage*
- *Business planning stage*
- *Fundraising guide*
- *Marketing*

The full scope of the app coverage positions them to be the dominant mobile apps for entrepreneurs.

<u>Analysis of the exective summary from the business plan for a mobile app:</u>

My goal with this executive summary was to clearly explain what the product was, and to make the business sound intriguing and unique to the reader to make them want to continue reading. To make it sound intriguing I emphasized the uniqueness of this project and how it can become a go-to tool for entrepreneurs. That would be a signal to the reader that this will be a big opportunity.

2. Your product or service

This is the section where you should be more precise about your product. Explain your company's product or service. Is it a website? A physical store or service? A widget or a mobile app? What is special and unique about it?

Explain why this product or service should exist, and why it is needed. Does it entertain? Does it make someone feel better? Does it solve a problem for someone? Does it teach something? What is the benefit of this product or service?

It may sound like a silly way to pose the question, but surprisingly many companies create a product or service that is not really needed, which causes difficulties when trying to sell, promote or getting people to use it.

Additionally, if your product or service is only needed a little bit, and doesn't solve a huge pain point and does not provide some great value, it may be difficult to get people to pay for it.

Lastly, but very importantly, unless your product or service is very self-explanatory, explain how your product achieves what it promises to achieve. Don't leave that question unanswered or vague.

Example of the product section of a business plan for a mobile app:

These are mobile apps on Android and iOS. There are 4 apps on Android and 4 apps on iOS. The apps help people plan, start and grow their businesses.

The reason there are 4 apps on each platform is that each of the 4 apps helps entrepreneurs with a specific stage of starting a business. The 4 apps cover:

1) Business ideas
2) Business planning
3) Fundraising
4) Marketing

Each of the 4 apps helps new businesses in these 4 ways:

1) *Software tool to help people plan and save their plans right on the app. People will be able to create small business plans, fundraising plans and marketing plans on the app.*
2) *Ability to plan parts of their business with business partners and invite their whole team to use the app with them.*
3) *Tutorials to teach the entrepreneurs about the business stage they are in: business ideas, business planning, marketing and raising money.*
4) *Live business coaching and advice provided by an expert. In most cases, until the app has sufficiently grown, to ensure quality of help, the coaching will be provided via text chat on the app by the founder, Alex Genadinik.*

<u>Analysis of the product section of a business plan for a mobile app:</u>

My goal for this section of the business plan was to clearly explain what the products are and how they help people. I tried to make the product sound intriguing or different to make the product sound compelling. I also wanted to paint the picture that these apps have potential to be dominant or best within their product category.

Even if your product is a commodity service like lawn care, you can still make it interesting and unique by highlighting something compelling about it. Maybe you design the lawns using cutting edge modern art principles, have award winning customer service, or use organic grass products. These are just examples to show that any product can have something unique about it - no matter how commoditized it might be.

3. What stage of the business are you in?

Are you in the idea stage? Or have you started your business, and maybe you have a prototype of your product? Or do you already have some revenue and a team, and your focus is on growth?

Do not get into too many specifics here. Simply help the reader understand where you are in the process of building a company. It will help the reader have context within which to read the rest of the business plan.

It makes a big difference if your company is just being planned, or if it is already established and has achieved some level of success. The further you are in starting and growing your business, the more credibility your strategies will often garner.

Even though it is better to be further ahead than not, don't be shy if you are just at the idea stage. It is OK to be at any stage, even the planning or the idea stage. Every successful company has at some point been in planning stages. Just be honest about where you are in the process of planning, starting or growing your business.

Example of the business stage section of a business plan for a mobile app:

- Founded in 2012
- 50-100% growth year over year in first 3 years
- 25% growth last year due to saturation on Android and lack of growth on iOS
- Next year focusing on iOS growth

- Over 1,000,000 downloads
- (Fictitious due to privacy) revenue last year: $125,000

Analysis of the business stage section of a business plan for a mobile app:

In my version of this section, I was able to outline a few years of progress since these apps are live. That gives the reader a sense of the trajectory of the business in addition to the company's current status.

This section will be much simpler for you to write if you are just starting your business. All you will have to say is that you are either in the planning stages, or mention some initial accomplishments you've achieved after starting.

If you are at the beginning stages of your business, the more you can say that you did the better you will look in the eyes of whoever is reading your business plan because many people who plan and discuss their businesses never actually start. The more you can separate yourself from those people the better.

Even if you have not started, you can talk about your market research, customer development (I'll explain what this is in a later chapter), or anything else you did before your business has started. Anything you actually did instead of sitting and dreaming about your business will give you a slight boost in credibility.

4. Your target market

It is easy and tempting to think that everyone can use your product, but that would be a mistake. Of course, you would like and encourage everyone to be your customer, but there are usually a few types of people for whom your product will be a better fit. Identifying who those people are and focusing on that particular consumer base will also help you better target your marketing and product usability efforts.

Especially in the beginning, try to understand who will be the ideal customers for your product. Once you identify your target consumer, effectively market your business to them, and get them to love your product, you can expand to other types of consumers.

You can identify potential customers by three things: demographics, psychographics, and geolocation.

Demographics are things like people's age, sex, income level, education level, marital status, whether they have children or not, whether they own a car or a house, and many other things that can be measured.

Psychographics are people's attributes that can't be measured precisely, but are still important. These are things like a person's desires, wants, hopes, fears, hobbies, interests, insecurities, mental blocks, different common emotions they are prone to, and even things like confusion and delusion.

Geolocation targeting is self explanatory. Some businesses draw clients from local areas and some businesses draw clients globally. A local liquor store draws most of its customers from the surrounding five block area while an average restaurant draws most of its customers from a slightly larger surrounding neighborhood area. A handyman business can attract customers from anywhere in an entire city or a few closest nearby cities because the handyman is able to travel there. And an online business can usually attract clients globally although some countries tend to be far better markets to target because they are wealthier and usually have more people who can spend money, or speak a language which is best suited to consume your product.

Let me give you a concrete example of how I identify a target market for a product of mine. The product is this free Android business planning mobile app, which might actually help you since it is on the same topic as this book, and is free. So feel welcome to download it:

https://play.google.com/store/apps/details?id=com.problemio

I'll explain what the geographic targeting, demographics, and psychographics are for the users of this app so that you can see my thought process for identifying them.

First let's cover the geographic targeting. The app is an English-only app so the best countries for this app are countries where there is a large base of English language speakers and Android users. These countries are USA, Canada, UK, Australia, South Africa, India, Indonesia, Malaysia, and a few other large countries that have large populations because even if a small percentage of people in those countries speak English, that would still make for a significant user base of English language speakers.

The demographics for this app are a little bit more nuanced. Most people who use apps are generally younger. Most entrepreneurs tend to be younger people. Most of the users for this app are under 30 years old, and often under 25 years old. They are usually not wealthy since usually younger people are less affluent than older people, and entrepreneurs are not known to be wealthy when they first start out either. The users for this app are almost always first time entrepreneurs, single, and often still in college, just out of college, or even in high school.

The psychographics are where things get interesting. What are the app users like as people? What do they need and want in life? Over time I have gotten to know my app users pretty well. Very often they aren't necessarily interested in starting a business as much as they just need to make some money. Usually that happens to people when they are in somewhat dire and stressful life circumstances. They need a advice and direction because they usually have no support or very little support in their business ventures or careers, and are generally very thankful when the app provides them with some support. Usually the kinds of businesses that people on my apps try to start are not too technical. Most of the businesses being planned on the app are different kinds of local services or other traditional businesses.

You see, by combining the geolocation, demographics and psychographics we can get to know a lot about the average app user. Once we have a deep understanding of our target customers, we can create a product that pleases them, and we can better understand how to promote our product to reach people who are in our target market.

WHAT NOT TO WRITE IN THE TARGET MARKET SECTION: don't write something like "everyone" or "all women" or "all men", or all people in some country or city. You have to show a much deeper understanding of your target consumer and their consumption behavior.

Since identifying your target market is such an important topic, let me leave you with a few more thoughts on it.

Understanding your consumer makes it easier and cheaper to

reach them in large volume with targeted marketing and advertising. It also makes it easier to create a product that better satisfies their needs, and is used by them in a manner that is convenient to them (important for product adoption and customer retention). It also helps you better understand your market size which enables you to make more accurate financial estimates.

Point to realize: narrowing down your target market to some specific group is not the same thing limiting as limiting the potential of your opportunity. Narrowing down is the process of identifying your ideal customers.

A common misunderstanding is thinking that targeting a certain demographic limits the total opportunity of the business. There are two reasons why this is a misleading line of thought:

1) Choosing a target market helps you focus your advertising efforts and optimize your product to make that certain group very pleased with it. It still means that you will take anyone as a customer if they want to be your customer. You are not rejecting customers. But by targeting a specific kind of customer, you are helping your business get the most out of a certain demographic of people who are best suited to be your customers.

2) If you start small with a sharper focus on a certain type of customer, it does not mean that you cannot grow bigger and expand out of that later. When your business is ready, you can target additional types of customers as you expand.

Another thing to note is your addressable market vs. overall market.

Within every market there is the total market. There is a subset of that market made up of people who are more likely to become your customers.

The total available or addressable market is the entire market in which your business is in. The target market for your start-up is the part of that total market that your start-up can realistically target.

If, for example, you are opening a fine dining restaurant, the overall market for people who visit restaurants is probably everyone in your city. But your target market is much narrower. The market that you can realistically target is only those people who like to eat the certain kind of food found that is served in your restaurant, can afford to eat out instead of dining at home, and most likely live within a 1-2 mile radius from your restaurant. Since in this example we are discussing a fine dining restaurant, the target demographic may also be over 30 (or even 40) years old.

Here is another example. The total United States shoe market is in the billions of dollars per year. But if you made a shoe which is a slipper for men, you could only sell that to a portion of men in United States.

It might be *tempting* to say that your target market is all men because there is nothing preventing all men from wearing slippers. But it would not be correct to say that your target market is all men. Many men hate wearing slippers, and it can very difficult to force kids and teens to wear slippers. Some men 18-45 years old might not like wearing slippers either because they might make them feel like a grandfather when they wear it. Plus, many people prefer to walk around their homes barefoot. Older men tend to wear slippers at home, but as a demographic, they shop least often because many elderly people live in poverty (or extreme saving mode), and can get items like slippers for free from various government help organizations. So it turns out that older people who would like your product the most, belong to a demographic that spends the least. And that is not a great situation.

The deeper you understand who behaves and spends in which particular ways, the better you will be able to estimate who you can sell to, and identify a target market that can be lucrative and realistic to go after.

Additionally, if you had said that your target market for slippers was all men, and if you tried to market the slippers to all men, that would result in quite a bit of a wasted money time and effort since reaching many of the men would do you no good since so many men don't wear slippers.

Example of the target market section of a business plan for a mobile app:

There is extensive customer research behind these apps. Until the apps reached 300,000 downloads, I (Alex Genadinik) answered every question asked on the apps. Not everyone asked a question, but many people did. Working with such a large sample set of entrepreneurs gave me an unprecedented view and understanding of the kinds of help they need, who exactly the people using my apps were, and the questions entrepreneurs have.

The idea for the app series is based directly on that customer research of working with such a high volume of entrepreneurs and their businesses.

Besides business ideas, business planning, marketing and fundraising, entrepreneurs also asked about legal and accounting topics. I decided not to cover legal and accounting topics directly within those apps. Instead, my plan is to partner with law and accounting firms to refer clients to them for a fee.

Demographics:

- *Largely under 35 years old (app users are usually younger)*
- *35% US, 10% India, 5% UK, 5% Canada, 5% South Africa, 4% Australia, 4% Malaysia, 3% Indonesia, the remaining 29% are in rest of the world, largely concentrated in the developing world since for many people there the smartphone is the only computing device they own.*
- *Low income*
- *Low education*
- *Not married*
- *No family*

Psychographics:

- *Don't necessarily need to start a business, just need to make money one way or another*
- *Largely low tech businesses*
- *Typically not the Silicon Valley start-up types*
- *Under financial stress and pressure*
- *Low confidence in business, maybe told by others not to do business*
- *Little family support*
- *No ability to make in-app purchases with a credit card due to being in the developing world. PayPal may be ok for some.*
- *They need a solution fast*
- *they have limited funds*
- *they prefer free*

<u>Analysis of the target market section of a business plan for a mobile app:</u>

I would like to emphasize that while you can get demographic data from market research and analytics software, to understand the psychographics of your customers you must be "nose deep" in their business. Find as many ways to talk to them as possible, and get to understand their needs. Notice that while I offered free help (I don't do that anymore) to my app users, it created a great product for them, but it also gave me unprecedented customer research. When it comes to your business, do your best to find as many ways as you can to talk to your current and potential customers. You will get great insights from those conversations, and those insights will help you create a better and more useful product that you can more easily promote.

5. Your target market size

This is the total dollar amount of the industry in which your business is in. Some markets are multi-billion dollar markets, some markets total hundreds or tens of millions of dollars. You have to show that you understand what your market is, and its size.

If you are building a company that sells something very niche, your market size may be small, but if you are selling computers or cars, your market size is in the tens or hundreds of billions of dollars, and is obviously very large.

This section also shows the reader that you have done some due diligence and understand the business environment in which you are operating.

WHAT NOT TO WRITE IN THIS SECTION: don't simply write something like huge, very big, millions, or billions. You must research and know the statistics of your industry, and not just provide vague approximations.

You have to be as specific as possible with the dollar amount of your market size. The closer you can get to the actual dollar amount of the market size, the better.

After you've noted the overall market size, narrow it down to your specific target market which is a subset of the total market.

Example of the market size section of a business plan for a mobile app:

The full potential for my apps will be reached when they dominate search and recommendation algorithms on both Android and iOS.

Just with dominating search, these apps can reach about 1,000,000 people per year.

Once the apps are widely recognized, they can get big publicity and by being featured in the Apple App Store and the Google Play store. That would result in 100,000-300,000 more downloads per year.

An average download generates $1.00 of revenue which means that at its peak these apps will generate $1,100,000 to $1,300,000 per year.

(I want to once again remind you that the financial data is fictitious because I keep the actual financial data private)

<u>Analysis of the market size section of a business plan for a mobile app:</u>

The challenge I faced when writing this section was that there is no research on the total market size for business apps. Because of that I extrapolated the full potential of my apps from their current data and made an educated estimate.

6. Marketing plan: how will you market to your target users

The marketing plan is arguably one of the most important sections of a business plan. It was one of our core three components in the 3-sentence business plan.

There are many ways to market a product or service, but not all marketing techniques work for all companies. Your marketing plan must outline how you will consistently reach your target market at scale required for your business to succeed, and convert them to clients.

You have to craft your marketing plan very carefully. If your marketing plan does not contain viable and effective strategies, you may spend your time and money making misguided marketing efforts which might result in your funds, effort and many months wasted without getting clients. Needless to say that many businesses don't recover from such errors and fail precisely due to having an ineffective marketing plan.

COMMON MISTAKE AND WHAT NOT TO SAY: If your marketing plan reads something like "I will promote my business by posting on Facebook, Twitter, and handing out flyers and business cards" then my initial guess would be that you are on your way to making a very common big mistake.

The marketing strategy of "I will promote my business by posting on Facebook, Twitter, and handing out flyers and business cards" is something that most first-time entrepreneurs and first-time marketers say. They say that not because this is the best way to promote their unique business, but simply because they don't know any better, and those strategies are the ones that come to mind and make sense to the inexperienced marketer.

If you want ideas that will be effective for promoting your business and help creating a good marketing plan, since I have extensive experience creating marketing plans for different kinds of businesses, I can do my best to help you if you reach out and email me. It does take some time to create a marketing strategy because it has to take your unique business situation into account. So please be clear and brief with your questions. Feel welcome to send your 3-sentence business plan to me so that I can understand your business at a high level. And hint-hint, if your email starts with something like "I love your book and I just left a nice review of it on Amazon" I'll appreciate that, and I'll put your questions to the front of the line.

I have also created a number of resources to help you become better as a marketer and create a better marketing plan.

Here is a very comprehensive YouTube video that will teach you how to create a marketing plan for your business for free since YouTube videos are free:

https://www.youtube.com/watch?v=ZXIDvVoOgOI

I also wrote a marketing plan book and created online video-based courses which can help you become better at marketing. At the end of this book I explain how you can get some of those for free as well.

For the sake of your business and your financial welfare, your marketing plan must be professional and effective because the growth of your business depends on it. Plus, whoever reads your marketing plan will put a lot of weight on it when evaluating your overall plan since they will understand the importance of it. A common way investors can spot an inexperienced entrepreneur is when they don't have an effective marketing plan.

Example of the marketing plan section of a business plan for a mobile app:

The marketing of these apps will be through

- *Mobile app store search (Apple App Store and Google Play Store)*
- *Publicity and PR*
- *Social sharing from people inviting business partners to help plan their businesses on the apps.*
- *My website Problemio.com*
- *Google search*
- *YouTube channel*
- *Podcast*
- *Facebook, Instagram and AdWords Ads*

Since for most apps, the bulk of their downloads comes from app store search, that is where I will concentrate.

Analysis of the marketing plan section of a business plan for a mobile app:

My apps have gotten 95% of their downloads from app store search. Another 4.9% of the downloads came from promoting them through various publicity and PR sources, social sharing, my YouTube channel and my website. I didn't try to create a podcast to promote my apps by paying for ads, but if I did, I imagine that it would have given my app a small bump.

The reason that this marketing plan is good is because that is precisely what works for most apps, and what worked for mine. The lesson here is that you have to identify the marketing strategies that work specifically for your unique business and situation. And if you've never promoted anything before, my advice is to get help with a marketing strategy before you start your business rather than after.

7. Revenue model

In this section you must outline how and when you will generate revenue. How many revenue streams will you have? What will be your strongest revenue stream?

There is quite a bit of confusion about the terms business model, revenue model and revenue stream. They often get mixed up. The term business model is often incorrectly used to express how your business generates revenue. As we covered earlier, a business model is something greater. A business model takes all the components of your business into account and evaluates how they work with one another. The revenue model is just a part of the business model, and a revenue model can have one or more revenue streams in it.

Now let's go over some of the most common revenue streams

and examine when and how they should be applied to your overall revenue model.

THE AD REVENUE STREAM

The ad revenue stream is the simplest revenue stream. All you do is create an ad, publish it on your website, billboard, or any other property, and you are set to go. But the truth is that your customers hate ads, and ignore them as much as possible. That makes ads so ineffective that they can only make a reasonable amount of money if the website, billboard, or other media on which they are placed gets a very high volume of views. And the per view revenue is typically atrociously low.

On the web, the most common place to get ads which you can put on your website is Google's AdSense.

http://www.google.com/adsense

For most sites, AdSense will earn somewhere from $5.00-$10.00 per 1,000 page views. A thousand page views is the common unit of measurement for ads. It is denoted by CPM.

If a typical CPM (cost per thousand views) is $5, then you need 10,000 views to make $50. To make $500 you need 100,000 page views. And to make $5,000 which is getting close to the vicinity of a middle class monthly salary for one person in United States, you need to generate one million page views which is extremely difficult for most websites.

If you decide to monetize your business with ads, your site will need to attract millions of people for you to be able to make any real money and grow your business. What you can do to increase your revenue potential is to think of another revenue stream that can work together with your ad revenue stream to improve results or replace it entirely.

One mistake I often see first-time entrepreneurs make is have a mismatch of business type to revenue stream choice. This often happens with the ad revenue stream because it can seem like such an obvious choice. But to be effective, The ad revenue stream needs many views and effective targeting. If you don't have a high volume website or business, the ad revenue stream might not be ideal for you.

AFFILIATE REVENUE STREAM

The affiliate revenue stream is a very popular one, especially on the web. With this revenue stream you become an affiliate reseller of products or services provided by another company. This works on the web by having the affiliate reseller place links to relevant products on their website, and collecting commission on the generated sales.

This can work together in conjunction with ads, or separately.

If you get it working well, selling affiliate products can sometimes make an order of magnitude more money than publishing ads. That isn't the case every time, and depends largely on your business niche, the kinds of products you are selling, and your audience. Pound for pound, selling affiliate products is more lucrative than publishing ads if you had to choose one over the other.

And again, I have a full course on affiliate marketing if you are interested in learning about that. You can learn how to get that course for free at the end of the book.

TRANSACTIONAL REVENUE STREAMS

A transactional revenue stream is one where you get paid directly in exchange for goods or services. This includes most kinds of commerce. Think about Amazon or any other online or offline store. Most traditional services also use the transactional revenue stream. For example doctor's offices, cleaning businesses, restaurants, etc.

The transactional revenue stream is a very simple and direct way to get get paid. It's strength is in simplicity and direct path to revenue. You sell goods or provide a service, and people pay you for that. There is no need for publishing ads, or referring people to some other affiliate websites or businesses, and there is no waiting or hoping for sales to be made elsewhere or down the line.

Usually there are two challenges for this kind of revenue stream. The first challenge is that people have to pay. Since they typically don't like to do that, they have to either really need whatever you will be selling, or you would have to perfect your sales. The second challenge is that as soon as something can be sold for a profit, many others usually jump on the opportunity, and the business environment becomes crowded and competitive, making it difficult to promote the business effectively, and bring in new customers in high volume.

Additionally, once there is competition, there begins to be price deterioration which causes everyone to make less money. Consumers love this because they get more options at cheaper prices, but this is bad for your business because you end up making less money.

Nevertheless, if you can sell something, that is a great option to have. You just have to beat all your competition.

Many people do not think of themselves as someone who can make a product, but I want to make the argument that very likely, you *are* able to make a product that you can sell.

There are many different kinds of products. There are written works like books that you can sell. There are arts and crafts that you can make at home and sell online. There are mobile apps or software products you can create on your own or outsource. You can even get into 3d printing and create 3d products that can be sold online. You can paint things, or make some kind of creative products. There are many different kinds of things you can make. Imagination is the limit. Just think of your talents. I am sure you will be able to come up with something great. An idea for a product may not come to you today, but if you think about it, a good idea for something you can create and sell will come to you sooner than you might think. Once you can create something, the great thing is that there is surely a way to sell it and get paid immediately.

SUBSCRIPTION-BASED REVENUE

This is a darling of business owners. Not only does this mean recurring and somewhat predictable revenue, but it also means that revenue can accumulate every month as you grow your subscriber base.

If you can maintain a higher sign-up rate than your unsubscribe rate, you will have a beautiful revenue growth graph that is always up and to the right, with more subscribers and revenue each month.

Plus, the dirty little secret of subscription-based revenue is that many people simply don't unsubscribe because they are lazy or uncertain of whether they want to completely cut off the service. Think about how many people maintain their gym memberships, but have not been to the gym in months (or years, ouch)

MAXIMIZING THE POTENTIAL OF ANY REVENUE STREAM YOU CHOOSE

There are three common ways to maximize the earnings from your revenue streams. You can charge more for your product, extend the duration of the relationship you have with each customer, and optimize the rate at which new people are converted into paying customers. Let's explore each of these in more detail.

As a business owner, you always want to think about how to extend the lifetime relationship you have with your customers. Let's consider the example of buying a car. Does your relationship with that car dealer end there? It doesn't. The dealer encourages you come in every 6 months for basic maintenance services. This gets you into a habit of going to that dealer. Then when it is time to buy your next car, you are likely going to consider buying from them again. Plus, any time you visit them, there are car accessories they can sell to you as well.

Let's consider a simple example of a blog that makes money with ads. If you visit the blog once, they will have one chance to make money from you by showing you ads. If you never come back, they lose the chance to show you more ads. But if you like the blog and become a daily reader, they can show you ads 365 more times that year. That is a difference in earnings by a multiple of 365 times!

If you look at almost any established business, you can notice a way in which that business tries to extend the length of the relationships with its clients. Even my business does it. For example, in my mobile apps there is an option to hire me as a business coach, and continue getting mentoring from me as you grow your business. In fact, if I can share with you how I think about my apps, I constantly think about two ways to improve my apps: how to make the user experience better, and how to make the apps something that people use every day in their business. The more I make the apps something that people use every day, the more I can help entrepreneurs and at the same time give myself a chance to make extra money from those engaged entrepreneurs.

Whether or not you are able to increase the duration of your relationship with your customers or not, you should also try to figure out how to charge more for your product or services. You can charge more by improving the quality of your offering, and by targeting a more affluent market in which people can afford to pay more for a higher level product or service. You can also add extra features to your product, which would enable you to raise the value of your product.

Lastly, what you should always be trying to do is to maximize the percentage of people who go from simply learning about your business to becoming paying clients of your business. To learn more about some strategies for how to do that, let's take a look at how to optimize your sales funnel.

A sales funnel is the series of steps a person goes through after they learn about your business to becoming a customer. Just about every business has a sales funnel. Improving the sales funnel improves the effectiveness of how your website or business converts people into paying clients. Optimizing your sales funnel can mean the difference between life and death for a business because the more effective your sales funnel is at converting visitors to buyers, the less money you need to spend on marketing. Having higher sales conversions makes your average cost to acquire a customer lower, and your business more profitable overall.

When you are marketing your business and getting the word out, you probably send people to your website or a physical location. That initial point where you tell people to go is the top of your sales funnel. Once people get to the top of your sales funnel, you need to have a very clear path for those people in order to purchase something, or perform some action that you want them to perform.

The first step to improving your sales funnel is to measure everything.

If you drive people to your website, you must use web analytics software to measure and understand what those website visitors are doing on your website. The most common free analytics software on the web is Google Analytics. You can sign up for it and start using it here:

http://www.google.com/analytics

Make sure that you use software analytics to understand what your users are doing on your website if you are not already using it. If you are not familiar with web analytics, you definitely need to be. It will help your business quite a bit, and it is an industry standard. If you don't use analytics software, you are literally "driving with your eyes closed" because you have no idea what people are doing on your website.

Web analytics will help you understand how many people visit your website, and what people are doing when they come to every page of your website. You need those website visitors to go to the next step of your sales funnel from whichever page they may be on. With analytics, you will be able to see whether people are taking the steps you need them to take or whether the funnel breaks down somewhere causing them to quit. Knowing what your website visitors are doing will give you insight into how to adjust the site in order to get more of your website visitors to take the right steps to progress further in your sales funnel.

By now you may be asking how you can increase the rate at which people move forward through the sales funnel. What you have to do is define a clear call to action (usually a big button somewhere on the page) letting people know that this is where they need to go. Once you have added your call to action, try experimenting with where on that page the call to action should be, and what text should surround that call to action to make it more enticing for the website visitors to click it. You should also experiment with different layouts of the page to see what kind of a layout, color scheme, and usability might give you better results.

The best way to experiment is to use something called AB testing. AB testing is a testing technique in which you have two or more versions of a web page. You then drive people to both versions of that page, and test which of the web pages or designs generates a higher percentage of people performing that action that you want them to do.

The version of the page which works best to get users to do what you want them to do is the one you keep on your site.

Another way to improve your sales funnel is to shorten it. You can create a single page that is optimized for a single action that you want people to take. That kind of a page is called a landing page because once you create that page, you can drive people to land on it. It typically produces satisfactory results because prior to driving people to it, you are able to extensively test its effectiveness, and only drive people to it once you are satisfied with how effective it is.

Landing pages are a great tool to help you minimize the steps in your sales funnel, and therefore increase conversion of website visitors to buyers. Less steps means less people veering off the desired path in your sales funnel.

Example of the revenue plan section of a business plan for a mobile app:

(note: the numbers here are fictitious due to privacy about my personal and business finances)

- In-app purchases of content
- In-app subscriptions to coaching
- Up-selling coaching services off the app
- Up-selling my books and online courses
- Selling affiliate products like website hosting for new businesses and legal and accounting services
- Sponsors

Annual revenue: $125,000

In-app purchases of content $45,000
In-app subscriptions to coaching $30,000
Up-selling coaching services off the app $20,000
Up-selling my books and online courses $10,000
Selling affiliate product like website hosting
for new businesses and legal and accounting
Services $10,000
Sponsors $10,000

Next year projected revenue: $161,000

```
In-app purchases of content  ........................ $60,000
In-app subscriptions to coaching  ................ $40,000
Up-selling coaching services off the app ....... $25,000
Up-selling my books and online courses ....... $12,000
Selling affiliate products like website hosting
for new businesses and legal and accounting
Services  .................................................... $12,000
Sponsors  .................................................. $12,000
```

Analysis of the revenue plan section of a business plan for a mobile app:

Just like in the marketing plan section of the business plan where I identified the most effective marketing strategies for my industry and product, I've identified the top revenue sources for apps and chose the ones that would be the best fit for my unique app.

The lesson here is that you have to understand your industry, how comparative companies usually generate revenue, take into account the uniqueness of your situation, and come up with the most effective ways to monetize your customers and retain them as customers as long as possible.

8. The finances

Before you start and as you grow your business, you must have a clear view of its overall financial picture. Maintaining a balance sheet or a cash flow statement can help you keep track and have a better understanding of the overall financial picture of your business.

Large businesses typically have accountants who work on this section of their business plan, but if your business is small or you are just starting your business, you can create a basic cash flow statement, and that can be sufficient.

Let's take a closer look at how you can create your own cash flow statement.

A cash flow statement is a financial statement that shows changes in balance sheet accounts and income affect cash (and cash equivalents), and breaks the analysis down to operating, investing, and financing activities.

That sounds complex, right? Let's simplify that definition. A cash flow statement for a new business is a glorified itemized list of ways cash (and cash equivalents) is coming in and out of your business.

For new businesses, I recommend creating two such statements since your cash flow will look very different before and after you open your business. The first cash flow statement will be for the time period before you open your business, and the second statement will have to do with cash flow after you open the business. Let's take a look at a small example.

Let's say that you are opening a restaurant in United States. First, let's focus on the cash flow before the business is open.

Some (not all) of the cash flows *out* of the business are:

- Renting of the physical space
- Legal and business registration fees
- Salaries of some early employees

- Remodeling of the space

The cash flows *into* the business will be from funding sources like investments, loans, grants, donations etc.

Now let's focus on the cash flow statement after the business has started. Some (not all) of the cash flows out are:

- Monthly rent
- Employee salaries
- Utilities
- Liability insurance
- Ingredients for the food
- Marketing costs

And the cash flows *into* the business are the different revenue streams the business may have.

The reason that creating this document is so important is that it gives you a clear sense of the financial picture for your business, and enables you to make financial projections. That enables you to understand how much money you will need to start and run your business until you reach desired milestones.

When you pitch your business to investors, having created a cash flow statement, you will know exactly how much money to ask for. Depending on the type of business you have, you can ask for enough money to get you to some milestone, or if you just need cash to get your business off the ground, you should secure about 9-16 months of financial runway after the business has started.

Example of the finance section of a business plan for a mobile app:

Costs:
- Under $2,000 per year in outsourcing for design and development of features that I don't have time to code
- Under $1,000 per year for marketing costs
- After the apps are built, 5 hours of my time per month

Profitability:
- In the fictitious finances of this business, that would be $123,000 annually since the only cost is design and minor outsourcing.

Operating profit:
- Since my business has only minimal other costs, after taxes on $120,000 (minus cost of design AND marketing AND accounting), I make $65,000.

Net profit:
- After I pay myself, $50,000 annually, the business profit is $15,000

Profit Margin

Net profit / revenue: $15,000 / $125,000 = 0.12

Note that if I paid myself less, my business would have been immediately more profitable and with a healthier margin:

Net profit / revenue: $35,000 / $125,000 = 0.28
Net profit / revenue: $65,000/ $125,000 = 0.52

Balance sheet (fictitious)

Assets:

Current assets:
- Cash in the bank $50,000
- Coaching clients payments owed to me: $3,000
- Total: $53,000

Fixed assets:
- Laptop: $1,000
- Office supplies and furniture: $1,000
- Trademark: $500
- Total: $2,500

Liabilities: None

Outsourcing I owe: $500

Equity = $55,500 - $500
$55,000

Analysis of the finance section of a business plan for a mobile app:

Definitions:
- Gross profit: income remaining after accounting of good sold
- Operating profit: subtracts additional costs of your business

Most businesses would also have a cash flow statement which is a list of the ways that cash comes in and out of your business. In this example I don't have that because I listed expenses here and revenues in an earlier section. So the information that would be present in a cash flow statement is there - just not specifically in a cash flow statement.

9. Unit economics overview

This is one of the most important sections of a business plan. This section outlines the details of each transaction. By focusing on the details of each transaction you can get insight into how profitable your business is on a per-transaction level.

Once you understand the finances of each transaction, you can look at possible transactions per day, month, or year and understand which areas of your business need to be improved so that scaling operations will be profitable.

Understanding the anatomy of the finances of a single transaction can give you a great sense of what is working well, and what needs to be improved in the business.

This section tends to be one of the more intimidating sections of a business plan, so here is an example:

Imagine you are selling a widget. You sell the widget for a certain price, but it takes you some amount of time and money to produce, market, and sell the widget, while incurring costs like paying your employees, rent, paying for materials, and other bills. So there are expenses to creating and selling the widget. Expenses are easier to calculate because most of them are fixed. Some of them are employee salary, rent, and cost of the materials to produce the widgets.

You have to figure out what it costs you to put a widget into the customer's hands, and what you will charge for the widget. That is a single transaction. Once you dissect a single transaction this way, is it profitable? Or does it lose money? There is more to understanding unit economics, but for this introductory tutorial, this is a good way to begin thinking about it.

Your job is to figure out the number of widgets you need to sell in order to 1) break even financially on a month to month basis, 2) turn a profit, 3) finance further business growth or reaching further business goals.

You should also consider whether selling as many widgets as you need in order to meet your financial goals is viable through your available marketing channels and the size of your target market.

Example of the unit economics section of a business plan for a mobile app:

Since the product is a digital product and 99% of my marketing is from free sources, there is no cost of goods or marketing costs. Every download brings in (fictitious) $0.10 on average LTV (lifetime value of a customer).

The LTV per customer is on par with other mobile app businesses. Most apps struggle to make money per customer, and make up for the lack of per customer revenue by generating many downloads.

Since this is a digital good, any revenue is pure profit.

How I will extend the lifetime customer value (LTV)

- I use a "catalog" model to extent LTV by offering many upsells in the apps. I list all of my 20 books and 100+ online courses so when one person buys one, and they like it, they might buy a few more.

- I offer a subscription service on one of the apps. If a

person subscribes for a year, that is 12 times more revenue than from a 1-time purchase, which represents a 1200% increase in revenue. A 2-year subscription represents a 2400% increase in revenue from the same customer, and so on as the subscription length grows.

- As one of the up-sells in the app, I offer long-term off-app business coaching which can generate thousands of dollars with the right client.

- I am working on supporting the customers better and having them use the app longer. I am working on increasing LTV by improving design, making features more useful and generally more beneficial to my users. Longer engagement will boost monetization per customer.

- Email collection and email marketing to get people to re-engage with the app.

Analysis of the unit economics section of a business plan for a mobile app:

Since the apps are free and there is no immediate transaction when people download the apps, for this kind of product the goal is to retain the user long-term, make them a superfan or a superuser to a point where they eventually warm up to the idea of paying for something on the apps. Once the app users warm up to the idea of engaging with paid options on the apps, the apps paid options are positioned in a way to optimize the purchasing options of the users.

10. Current team

Provide brief professional backgrounds of each of the members of your executive team, and discuss the current size of the team. Explain why each team member's experience is the right fit for this business. Bonus points if the team has worked together before, and if members of the team have deep experience in the industry in which your business is in. Additionally, if you have great mentors or advisers, you should add them to this section as well.

Example of the current team section of a business plan for a mobile app:

This is a single founder business.

Alex Genadinik: 5+ years software engineering, 10+ years marketing, 5+ years product creation, successful entrepreneur.

Analysis of the current team section of a business plan for a mobile app:

This section is simple. All you have to do is list the top members of your team, any board members, or notable advisors or mentors.

11. Your competition

It is important to understand the competitors in your business environment. Your competitors are to be respected, understood, and learned from. You need to understand why they are successful as well as their shortcomings. Wherever they fail may be an opportunity for your business to pick up and differentiate from them, and carve out a niche for your business. Wherever your competition is strong is an opportunity to learn from them. You do not need to be better than your competitors in everything, but you do need to understand how your business will be different, and what section of the target market your approach may satisfy better. You also need to have strategies for competing with your competitors moving forward.

WHAT NOT TO DO: Don't over-focus or obsess about your competitors. There will always be someone competing with you. Understand and learn from your competitors, but focus on making your own business better. In the beginning, there are far more dangerous things than competition. New businesses are much more likely to die from basic implosion if they do not offer a great product or service, and sell it effectively.

Example of the competition section of a business plan for a mobile app:

-   Other business plan templating apps. My apps are different in that they help entrepreneurs create higher quality business plans by educating entrepreneurs and discouraging an over-reliance on templates which fill up the business plan with reused content full of buzzwords.

-   Gimmicky business plan apps that promise business plans in 5 minutes. Since my apps focus on the quality of the business plan and entrepreneur education, the business plans created with my apps are much better.

-   Pen and paper planners. My apps are more portable,

offer cloud storage for natural backup, and can be used to plan a business with partners remotely.

- Business card apps, business news apps, productivity apps and other big budget apps. These apps are not direct competitors, but I end up having to compete with them for similar searches in the Apple App Store and Google Play Store.

Analysis of the competition section of a business plan for a mobile app:

The right thing to do in this section is to list actual competitor products or companies. I didn't list any specific companies because I didn't want to give them any extra promotion in my book. Instead, I gave types of companies, products or consumer behavior. In your actual business plan, try to give examples of competitive companies, products and user behaviors, and explain how you set yourself apart from them.

12. Previous investors and funding

Give an overview of how your business has been funded so far. Depending on who will be reading your business plan, you can take out or add various sensitive information from this section (as well as other sensitive financial information throughout your business plan).

Example of the funding section of a business plan for a mobile app:

There is no previous funding. The apps were self-funded and created by Alex Genadinik who retains 100% ownership.

Analysis of the funding section of a business plan for a mobile app:

This section is easy to write, but extremely difficult to get right in the real world as you build your business because it is extremely stressful and difficult to create your business without necessary funding. But the problem with funding, of course, is that to get it you sometimes have to give away a part of your company ownership and with that some of the decision making power. You also don't want to go into personal debt to start a business.

In most cases, while this is understandably difficult to create a business without raising money, it is considered good to go as long as possible without seeking outside funding. It leaves you in control of your business and without debt to anyone.

In the early stages of me creating these apps I did approach some investors. Luckily they said no, and now I have all the decision making power, collect all the revenue, and don't need to make strategy decisions that investors would want to force on me in order to get a quick return on their investment.

13. What I am looking for

If you are handing the business plan to someone, you may want to add a section explaining why you are writing the business plan. Are you raising money? Are you hiring employees? If you are seeking something like funding or anything else, use this section as a good closing to your business plan. If the reader got this far, they are likely interested. Let them know how they can involved.

Example of the "what I am looking for" section of a business plan for a mobile app:

My company is looking to get into a start-up incubator, and get access to development and app usability experts. That help will take the 4-app series to the next level in terms of quality and help it dominate in the app stores. It will cause a doubling or tripling of downloads and revenue.

Analysis of the "what I am looking for" section of a business plan for a mobile app:

In my case I don't need money. I need very high level and very senior kind of advice on important details of my apps. Most people create a business plan because they need an investment or a loan.

Additionally, notice that in my example of this section, I also gave the milestone I am trying to reach with the help I am trying to get with this business plan.

14. Business plan appendix

If you have sensitive information in your business plan like any private financial data, investor information or business secrets, you can place them in the appendix section of a business plan. The purpose of having an appendix is for you to be able to easily add and remove sensitive information from your business plan, depending on who you will be showing the business plan to.

Example of the appendix section of a business plan for a mobile app:

My business plan example didn't have an appendix because I

put all the financial information in the body of the business plan. In your case you have the choice to move that information to this section.

CHAPTER 5: BUSINESS PLAN THOUGHT PROCESS EXAMPLES

"Intuition is a suspension of logic due to impatience."

- Rita Mae Brown

1. My initial business planning thought process when evaluating new business ideas

This is a fun section where I want to share with you my own mental process, and the logical steps I go through to evaluate a new business idea with a rudimentary business plan that I construct in my mind.

Keep in mind that I am not always right, and this is just my own thought process.

Also please keep in mind that this is just my mind. In my mind I am allowed to be a little bit sarcastic and possibly a little bit too realistic. So please bare with me.

Idea 1:

I love travel and I want to create a travel blog.

My thought process 1:

Travel is a great industry, but you will be competing against many multi-billion dollar companies so you must find a very smart niche or differentiation within the travel industry. Some examples of niches or differentiation can be travel in specific places or specific kind of travel like backpacking or luxury travel. If the person with this business idea has not thought about the niche too deeply, I know that there isn't much of a business idea there at all, and it becomes difficult to take the conversation too seriously.

If the person telling me this idea did choose a good niche, I proceed to think about how they will promote their business and whether they will be able to stand out within that niche. Will social media make sense to promote this business? Or will it be search engine marketing or YouTube or something else that will make for a great marketing strategy for this business? If none of the marketing strategies feel natural of "doable" and instead feel like they might be too competitive, it is a red flag. If I see a red flag like that, I begin to brainstorm changes to the initial idea and further differentiation until there appears a natural way to promote the business which will lead to a significant enough amount of traffic and clients.

Since the idea is travel, the revenue model does not concern me too much because in this industry the difficult part is to get high quality traffic with enough volume. Once you get the traffic, there are many potentially good ways to generate revenue from that traffic so I am not too worried about how the revenue will be generated. I am more concerned with whether there will be a realistic marketing strategy.

Idea 2:

New kind of a mobile app either for photos or social media or games.

My thought process 2:

This is another very common business idea that I see. What do you think these kinds of apps all have in common? I'll give you a few seconds to think about it 1...2...3 ok I hope you have your answer.

The thing these app ideas all have in common is that they are in incredibly competitive niches where their top competitors are multi-billion dollar businesses which happen to also be loved by their current user bases. The business ideas for new apps in these crowded spaces have little chance of being successful even if they are great apps. The competition is just too stiff.

Idea 3:

Local lawn care business or other kinds of local service businesses.

My thought process 3:

I actually love local service businesses. A local business is typically one that serves some local area. Such businesses can range from home improvement to restaurants to various medical offices to car washes to different kinds of stores.

I like many such businesses because all they have to do is provide a good service and beat out other local companies when it comes to marketing and promotion. If you consider how much easier it is to out-market other local businesses that are similar to yours than it is to out-market your competition in businesses that compete with businesses all over the world like apps, travel and other large industries, you will see that it is infinitely easier to beat your competition in a local market.

Idea 4:

A restaurant.

My thought process 4:

This is one local service that is truly difficult to start and turn into a successful business. You need a very substantial amount of money, countless licenses and permits just to open this kind of a business. After you open it, it typically takes months (if it ever happens) before this kind of a business breaks even and turns a profit. Not to mention that you will be working 6 or 7 day weeks and long hours every day. This is one business that I urge people to do extensive research on before opening.

Most people are saved from the mistake of starting a

restaurant by the simple fact that they don't have the funds for it, which makes them simply abandon their idea. But if you happen to be able to get the money to start a restaurant, be very-very careful, get a lot of coaching and guidance from someone who has opened a successful restaurant before, or partner with someone who has extensive experience in this industry.

Idea 5:

Affiliate marketing or making money online.

My thought process 5:

These days I talk to at least one (usually more) entrepreneur per week who has mistaken and confused notions they were given by someone else on the Internet about how easy it will be for them to make money online with affiliate marketing.

The idea of making money online has all the promises of a nice and simple life where you work very little, sit back while collecting a paycheck, and quit your 9-5 job and the daily commute to get there. People who struggle at their 9-5 jobs for a variety of reasons or just want to do something more creative with their lives tend to fall for this promise and embark on businesses that promise to make money online. Affiliate marketing tends to be one of the most common type of online business because it requires no skills, product or services. It is predicated on reselling products or services made by someone else.

It is possible to make a good living by working online. I know this firsthand because I do it myself. But I will be the first to say that for most people it takes A LOT of hard work and quite a bit of struggle before making a good living. So don't get fooled by other online marketers promising you to make money online quickly and easily.

You know what they say, if it is too good to be true, it probably is.

My advice is to approach this business just like you would any other. Plan out every aspect of your new online venture, make sure all parts of the strategy fit well with one another, and get quality and honest coaching in areas where you are new. And whatever you do, don't fall or try to look for get rich turnkey strategies. They will typically make someone else rich and you in worse financial shape than you were when you started.

Idea 6:

Any other new business idea.

My thought process 6:

When I hear a new business idea, here are the things I immediately ask myself. It is a little vetting process that I have when considering any new business idea:

- Am I actually interested in being in this business long-term? Am I interested in this industry?
- Can this product/service be built or delivered relatively cheaply and quickly with enough quality necessitated by the market in which it is in?
- How can I market-test it cheaply and quickly?
- Is the target demographic a lucrative one?
- Is there a big market for it?
- Does it solve a very big need?

- What are the natural marketing strategies for it?
- How long will the marketing take to begin working?
- Can this be done profitably?
- Is this business big enough for me to "make it big?" Or another way to phrase it is: if this business succeeds, will it make me enough money to retire or be able to move on to other things I want to do in my life?

With these questions I am trying to size up the risk, the viability of the business, the possibilities for growth, and whether it will be lucrative. That's the quick version of my little test.

CHAPTER 6: BUSINESS PLANNING MISTAKES & EXERCISES TO OVERCOME THOSE MISTAKES

"How much you can learn when you fail determines how far you will go into achieving your goals."

- Roy Bennett

Perhaps the biggest mistake anyone can make is to think that they are fine the way they are. From years of experience, I have developed a mantra of sorts for myself:

Everything can always be better.

If you are not making an effort to improve every aspect of your product and business, guess what, your competitors are! My best advice that I can give you that I give myself every day is to keep working on yourself and making yourself better at everything you do. It isn't easy to improve because it requires constant practice and learning, but do your best do everything you do well. You product or service quality will be a big part of your success.

Just make sure not to let your quest for perfection stop you from starting or launching. A good rule of thumb is to start/launch early and continuously work to improve over time.

Now let's cover other common entrepreneur mistakes that I hope you never make.

Mistake 1:

Don't use the process of writing the business plan as a way to put off and procrastinate on starting your actual business. I see many people deliberately and perpetually remain in the planning and research phase of their business. Please don't do this. At some point you must start doing the actual work your business requires.

Exercise 1:

Give yourself a planning and research deadline. Make a list of things you will begin to actually do for your business after the planning deadline expires.

You can and should continue to plan, strategize, and research different aspects of your business after that deadline, but use that deadline as a point after which at least 50% of your effort on your business will be actual work instead of just research and planning.

Mistake 2:

Many people find the finance section of the business confusing, and put it off. You will need to face this at some point. You can't hide from it for long. It is much better if you face this before you start your business instead of having to do it after you've started and made financial mistakes that could have been avoided if they were caught during the planning stage of your business.

Exercise 2:

Make a cash flow statement. Do you recall this from the finance part of the business plan and the business plan example? If not, it is okay. Let's go over it again. You can do this on a piece of paper or an Excel spreadsheet. Use whatever you feel comfortable with. Just be sure to recycle the paper once you are done with it.

Once you have your piece of paper or Excel ready, simply make two columns. One column is for a list of ways that money comes into your business, and the other column is for ways that money comes out of your business. You can do this if your business has already started, or if you are just planning it. Try to think of as many items for each column as possible.

Over time, you will have items to add and remove from this list, and the dollar amounts will become more accurate as you keep researching different aspects of your business and after you get started with it.

The cash flow statement is the first simple way to get your finances organized. It is easy to create and maintain.

Mistake 3:

A common mistake people make is not having another person look at the business plan to find mistakes or flaws in strategy.

Having someone look over your business plan is easy to do. It can help you catch costly mistakes. Those easily preventable mistakes can be very costly once you begin executing your business strategy if you came up with a bad plan of action. It can also be costly if you are planning to give your business plan to an investor or some organization.

A second pair of eyes can identify mistakes that you may have missed. If the business plan is important for you, have another person (or multiple people) read it over.

Exercise 3:

Look for an experienced business person to talk to you about your overall strategy and read your business plan. In most cases this would not be free because experienced business people are busy and reading someone else's business plan is not fun, but if you are serious about your business, if you can negotiate a reasonable price for yourself, it can be very worthwhile.

If you can't find business experts to give you feedback about your plan, the next best source of feedback are your business peers.

With all that in mind, don't forget that I offered to take a look at your 3-sentence business plan and give you feedback.

Mistake 4:

Getting someone else to write your business plan for you is a very common mistake. I can understand the temptation for this since writing a business plan can be confusing, frustrating, and let's face it, pretty boring.

But think about what will happen if someone else who doesn't truly understand your business plan writes your business plan for you. It will be a generic, mostly copy and paste plan that they probably got from somewhere else. By this point of the book, I hope it has become clear that a good business plan should take your unique situation into account. Another person simply doesn't know all the details. Another person will probably use some generic template and fill in largely generic content.

Exercise 4:

Write the business plan on your own, and get coaching or mentoring to help you with the difficult parts if you are stuck. A good coach or mentor can assist you in writing your business plan, listen to your ideas, and take many of the unique elements of your business and overall situation into account when helping you create the best possible business plan.

Another amazing benefit of having a mentor or business coach help you write your business plan alongside you is that when they come across potential pitfalls, they can discuss those issues with you right then and there, and actually improve the overall strategy on the fly.

And again, please don't think that I am suggesting that I should be this mentor or coach. I am NOT trying to sell you any services here. I am just trying to suggest what I honestly think is the best way to come up with a great business plan for you. My goal is to help you succeed.

Mistake 5:

Overly optimistic growth projections. I talk to many new entrepreneurs who talk my ear off about how great their idea is, how unique it is, and how it will revolutionize their industry and make them successful. It is good to dream big, but for most businesses that isn't how things play out. There is a lot of hardship before you can get to such a good place, and a bit of realistic thinking is also needed.

Exercise 5:

I love the idea of dreaming big so I don't want to tell you not to do that. But here is an exercise for you that might help you find a good balance between dreaming big and reality. Try to get feedback on your business idea from business peers and experts. When you get feedback, be sure to do more listening than talking. Don't be defensive if you hear something negative. Try to really hear and respectfully consider what people have to say. That will be a good balance for your big dreams. You don't have to do what people tell you or follow their advice, but it is good to hear different opinions so that you can have a wide perspective of the situation.

Mistake 6:

I see many first-time entrepreneurs try to have their business be all things to all people. When asked who their ideal customer is, they often say that everyone can be an ideal customer. This is almost never the case. You must have a very specific kind of a customer in mind in order to be able to truly satisfy them with your product and reach them with your marketing.

Exercise 6:

Try to talk to people who you think might be your customers and get their feedback on whether they need your product or service, whether they would buy it, and get their reasons for why yes and why not. This will help you develop a greater sense for who your potential customers truly are, and who aren't.

Mistake 7:

Don't make your business plan overly long. Don't use overly complicated vocabulary or sentence structure, and don't make the business plan borning. Your readers are human. Keep your business plan flowing well so that your readers don't quit reading it out of boredom and don't think less of you because you are incorrectly using complicated words. Also make sure to avoid too many buzzwords.

Exercise 7:

It is fairly simple to fix this. Simply re-read your business plan after you are done to see how it reads. Take out any mistakes you notice. Also take out any flowery language or unnecessary information. You can also ask a friend or hire an editor to read your business plan to help you make it more grammatically correct and easier to read.

Let me give you a pertinent example. This is my 3rd edition of this book which means that I've re-written it more times than that. Despite so many re-writes, I still find many sentences and paragraphs that can be restructured to make them shorter in length and more direct in meaning. The same will be true for your business plan if you edit it well.

Mistake 8:

Mistakes 6 and 5 are the kinds of things that will lead you to make another mistake, and that is to overestimate your target market.

Exercise 8:

Same as exercises 5 and 6, make sure you get the right feedback about your business ideas from different people in your industry and potential customers. There will be a section later in this book that will go over some good practices for how to get feedback.

Mistake 9:

Another common mistake is to fail to understand your competition. Many first time entrepreneurs have a tendency to say that there is no competition or that they are better than their competition. But if you are just starting out, probably everyone else who is currently in business is better.

Exercise 9:

Try to search Google for products similar to yours. I am always surprised by how many entrepreneurs don't actually do this or just Google something once, conveniently don't find anything noteworthy and forget it. Make sure to Google extensively and look for competitors using different searches.

Another way to find your competitors is by asking your potential customers about them. When you talk to your potential customers, ask them how they currently solve the need that your business will help them solve. In their answer and ensuing conversation, they might tell you who your competitors are.

Mistake 10:

One mistake I see young people make is that they often come to me after falling for some make money quick, get rich online scheme.

While it is very possible to make money online, few people are actually successful at it. And I don't know anyone who was able to do it quickly without too much work.

In my own experience, I did end up making a significant amount of money online. But it took years of struggle and trial and error before I got enough experience, knowledge and skills to be able to do that.

Exercise 10:

Try to build a network (sometimes called a mastermind) of entrepreneurs just like you who may be just starting out. Your group can be as small as two and as big as ten people who would commit to meet on a regular basis and share insights and help one another. This may help you see what your fellow entrepreneurs are going through so that you don't fall into make money quick schemes or other bad mistakes, and they might be able to help you spot poor decisions.

Bonus mistake:

Choosing the wrong business niche is another big and common mistake.

Bonus exercise:

We will spend the next chapter on this exact topic because the niche or differentiation you choose for your business is the foundation for everything you do moving forward, which makes choosing the right niche monumentally important.

CHAPTER 7: CHOOSING THE RIGHT BUSINESS NICHE

"If everybody is doing it one way, there's a good chance you can find your niche by going exactly in the opposite direction."

-   Sam Walton

I have written another book about choosing a business niche since it is such an important topic. This chapter is an excerpt from that book.

1. What is a business niche

A business niche is a subset of a market that a product or service might be focused on targeting in order to stand out or differentiate itself from the rest of the competition in that market.

2. Why you need a business niche

There are a few reasons to choose your business niche:

i. When first starting a business it helps you to find an area within large industries where you can be competitive.
ii. It helps you find a specialization within your industry so that people can refer others to you according to your specialization.
iii. It gives you a manageable and realistic target to achieve when first starting out without having to spread yourself too thin.
iv. It helps you focus your business strategy and marketing efforts.
v. It helps you differentiate from more established competitors in your industry.

3. Looking outside vs. looking inside yourself

If you are looking for niche ideas, you can certainly look at popular magazines, book topics, TV shows and other things in your daily life. Everywhere you look, you will get plenty of ideas for large and lucrative industries.

But in my opinion, it is far more powerful to first take a deep look inside yourself and examine your strengths and passions when looking for a good niche to choose. I find it more effective to work from an understanding of who you are and what drives you.

Once you identify a business area that you want to get into because it will be fulfilling to you as a human being, it is important to evaluate your business ideas or niche ideas with real world criteria. But before that, in my opinion, it is always important to look inside yourself first.

4. Additional tips on finding a business niche

The first thing you must do when choosing your niche is to follow your passion. Yes, I know that this sounds cheesy. Let me expand on that to make it a little less cheesy.

Most people's passions are fun things like travel, music or just sleeping or relaxing. That hardly helps because that leaves many boring industries that almost no one would ever get into if everyone just followed their passion. So instead of "follow your passion" let's change that to at least "have a strong interest in the industry in which you decide to start your business." And by the way, if your passion is just to create a business or to put food on the table for your family, that might be good enough.

The reason people say "follow your passion" is that working in an area you are passionate about gives you intrinsic motivation to work harder, longer, and to forge forward during challenging times. Try to identify what your strongest long-term motivations are, and start thinking about what businesses to get into from those areas of interest.

After identifying your passions or strong interests, the next thing to do is to start evaluating your personal strengths. From all the things you are passionate about, what are you also strong in? These strengths will give you a natural advantage when running your company.

Some strengths can be industry knowledge and experience,

ability to work alone, ability to build and manage teams, ability to network and leverage business connections, ability to take rejection, creativity, ability to raise money, and many more things that you can bring to the business to give it an advantage.

Similarly, consider your previous work experience and education. Is there something within your work history or education that you can bring to the business and use it as an advantage?

If you have industry experience, that is a huge advantage that you can bring to your business. In fact, if you don't have experience or industry knowledge, your first three to nine months of starting your business will be a huge learning experience which will be a very big disadvantage.

Just like you should carve out your business niche out of your strengths, you should also make sure to avoid starting businesses which will expose your weaknesses. For example, if you aren't a people person, maybe don't start a customer facing business. And if you don't know how to write software, trying to get into a technical business or a mobile app business would immediately put you at a disadvantage when compared to engineers starting a similar business. Having a disadvantage does not mean that your business will necessarily fail. It just means that it will be that much more difficult to succeed.

The next thing to consider when choosing a niche is whether you will have to initially build out a team to start a business in the niche, or whether you already have many of the necessary skills. As your business grows, you will hire and outsource many parts of your business. But in the beginning, you or someone on your founding team should be able to do many of the tasks needed by your business. You simply won't have the resources to hire and outsource everything, nor should you do that at first. My advice is to have your hand on the pulse of as many parts of your business as possible so that you can understand the ins and outs of every part of it.

For example, if you want to make a mobile app, it makes a big difference whether you can program the app on your own or not. Since I know how to program, I have an advantage over many people because I can make the app for free whereas someone who doesn't know how to program apps would have to pay someone else $10,000 or $20,000 to get the app developed and even more money to maintain and improve over time. That is a huge advantage for a person who knows how to make apps right from the start.

Of course, there are levels of advantages. For example, even if I can make an app, a well-funded start-up that has a whole team of engineers and designers can make a much better app in a shorter amount of time than I can.

Another point you want to consider when choosing a business niche is how competitive the business and marketing environment in it will be. If you are in the travel industry for example, that is a very competitive industry. When you start a business in such a big industry to be competitive, you have to find a niche within that big industry. One way you can niche down in the travel industry is by geolocation. One possible idea is to niche down to travel in United States. But that is still very competitive. So you might have to niche down to a specific kind of travel like backpacking or luxury travel, and maybe within even a smaller geographic area. That would be a far less competitive environment for you than trying to compete in the more competitive greater niches within your industry.

Of course, you also want to consider whether the small niche you choose is still big enough to help you achieve your financial goals for your business. If you niche down far enough that the niche becomes tiny, there may not be enough potential clients in it or enough money to be made for you to achieve your financial goals.

There is a famous blog post on this issue by Mark Suster who is a very well known and respected venture capitalist. The article is here:

http://www.bothsidesofthetable.com/2009/09/16/most-startups -should-be-deer-hunters/

To summarize the article, Mark talks about three kinds of markets you can take on. He refers to these markets as an elephant, a deer and a rabbit. A gigantic and competitive market is like an elephant. It is huge with potential for big reward, but difficult to overcome. A market that is too tiny is like a rabbit. Even if you hunt it and kill it, there isn't that much meat on it. So a deer sized niche is a perfect size. It is not too big to kill, and the reward is a good size.

By the way, I am only using hunting as an analogy. I love animals and I am actually against hunting. As an analogy, hunting makes sense.

When you are looking for your niche, try to aim for a deer-sized niche. It doesn't have to mean that you will always stay in this niche. Once you find success in any niche, you can always grow out of it, and move into bigger niches, but you must start somewhere manageable.

Another point you want to consider when choosing a business

niche or a business idea is your realistic goals for your life. Your business should enable you to reach your goals. If your goals aren't astronomical, you may not have to go after the most competitive or challenging business ideas in order to have your business get you to your financial goals.

Once you identify a business idea or an industry niche to pursue, try to consider how easy or difficult it will be to promote that business. Some types of businesses lend themselves well to certain types of marketing, but other types of businesses have fewer effective ways in which they can be promoted.

It does take an experienced marketer to be able to determine what business ideas are easy to promote and which are not. If you are not an experienced marketer, as one of my free gifts to you that I mention at the end of the book, I can give you feedback on your business idea and try to help you understand if it is a good business to get into. At the end of this book there is a section where you can read more about the free offers I made available for you.

Here are a few things to ask yourself when evaluating how easy or difficult a business idea is to promote. Is the business the kind of business that people search for on Google? Can it generate publicity from its uniqueness? Or can it go viral from social sharing?

The same sort of an evaluation process applies to monetization strategies that can apply to your business. Some business types have many natural ways in which they can generate revenue while others don't have as many natural ways in which they can be monetized. Again, if you aren't sure, before you start your business, this is a good thing to get advice on from a coach or from someone experienced in these issues. You don't want to get into a business in which it will be difficult to generate revenue.

Another thing to consider when choosing a niche is whether you already have a habit of dabbling in that space or area of interest.

Habits are scientifically proven to help people stick with something. A habit may be exercise or it may be working on your business. The power of habit is that it makes feel effortless, and allows us to keep doing it longer. So if you will spend years working on your business, having a habit of dabbling in something or regularly being in an environment that makes doing something easier increases your chances of success.

5. My own mistake when choosing a business niche

When I started my first business, I had no idea what business to get into. There was no one to teach me or advise me. There wasn't a book like this one, and there wasn't an online course I could learn from. When I was just starting out there wasn't even a YouTube! YouTube the company had not even been started yet. I guess I am old.

Since I had no help or guidance, I had to learn by making my own mistakes. And when you are new in business, everyone who knows at least a little bit about business seems like some sort of a great expert. At least that was how they seemed to me. One day I met someone who professed to be a "business guy" or an "idea guy" and since I didn't know how to tell whether they were good business people or not, I took his advice.

This person advised me to apply some of the technology I was working on at the time to the fashion industry. Since you don't know me, let me be honest with you: I have no natural interest in fashion and know nothing about it. This was absolutely the wrong industry for me to get into.

Take a second and think back to an earlier part of this book when I suggested that you should pursue a niche that you know something about. I didn't have that advice or insight when I was first starting out so I took this "business person's" advice and got into the fashion industry and focused on shoes as my business niche.

I hope a red flag just went off in your mind screaming that the shoe industry is still too large of a niche, and that I should have niched down further. Unfortunately, such a red flag did not go off in my head, and I plowed into the shoe market without knowing anything about it.

That mistake led me to fumble around in the fashion industry for a few months until the project failed. I learned a lot, but the outcome wasn't what I was hoping for. I was starting from zero in that industry with below average knowledge and below average interest in that industry. Everything was a first for me, and without good mentors I had no chance.

I wish I understood then that I needed to get into a niche in which I had knowledge, passion and experience. That is why I am sharing this with you now - so you don't make the same mistake that I did.

If you think that I was done making niche-choosing mistakes, I wasn't. For my next business I started a group hiking website. I like hiking. I can't say it was my "passion" but I certainly liked it and knew more about it than I knew about fashion.

The problem I ran into was not having a good marketing strategy. I originally tried to start it on a national level in United States. But it was just too difficult to get hike organizers to start using the website in different parts of the country. I then changed direction and shifted my niche to target a hyper-local area of Northern California and mainly San Francisco.

The problem with that niche was that it was too small to generate a significant amount of money through my initially conceived monetization strategy which was ads.

To succeed with the business I had to change direction again. This time the business turned into me organizing fun, themed outdoor hikes. Because the events were interesting and themed, I was able to charge people money to attend, and I was able to get local publicity and many attendees. That business turned out to be a nice one after I learned how to get it to bring in enough revenue. It was okay as a tiny self-run business, but it was never going to become a multi-million dollar business that would fulfill my hopes for it because it was difficult to scale. It did have some success, but not enough so ultimately I had to move on.

You see how many niches I had to try out throughout my journey, with none of them being perfect enough. It would have saved me many headaches and time if I planned better before I started that business.

6. How to brainstorm business ideas

It is great to get expert feedback and advice about your business ideas, but you don't always have access to experts.

If you can't get advice from an expert, you can still refine your initial idea by brainstorming it with peers.

Let me share with you how I like to brainstorm business ideas. You can use this method with a friend or on your own.

Whenever you get a business idea, you must ask questions about this idea. One of the questions might be whether the founding team (probably just you on day one) has the skills to do the work. If you can do or learn to do the work, you can save money by not having to hire additional workers. If not, you will need to hire help, which is an extra cost. You should also ask how you will promote this business. Do you have marketing expertise on the team or will that have to be outsourced? Also ask yourself whether the competitive business landscape for your idea is reasonable or whether it might be too difficult to stand out.

What happens during the asking of these common questions is that they may expose weaknesses in your overall strategy. Once you find the weaknesses in your business strategy, it can be adjusted to make the overall idea work. Sometimes when a part of the business strategy is adjusted, it misaligns other parts of the business strategy and you have to go back and ask the questions you've asked to make sure that the answers to them still make sense with the newly readjusted business strategy.

Here is a list of questions to ask:

- How will you promote the business?
- How will it make money?
- Does it target an affluent consumer base?
- How big is the market?
- Will you be able to compete in the current market?

- Will your founding team be able to bring this idea to market? What necessary skills is the founding team is missing?
- How long will it realistically take to get this business to succeed? Do you have that amount of time to work on this idea?
- If not, how far will you have to niche down in order to make the idea simpler and more feasible?
- If you have to niche down and change strategy, will the questions above still have the same answers? Sometimes they don't, and strategy needs to be adjusted further.

7. Have real conversations to get real feedback about your business

Once you picked a niche and an idea, and brainstormed it on your own to find areas where the idea might be weak, the next thing to do is to begin gathering feedback from different people.

You can get feedback from friends and family, business peers, people who you think might be potential clients, and industry professionals and experts.

Friends and family are great because they are almost always available to you. The problem with getting business feedback from them is that they don't necessarily understand business or the industry in which your business is in.

Business peers are good to talk to as well. But the problem with getting advice from business peers is that they might also be in the early stages of becoming entrepreneurs and their insights might not be that strong.

Note of caution: when you talk to friends and family, many of them will say something like "that sounds great" or "that sounds awesome" in their support for you. Don't fall for that as a positive sign about your business idea. Those nice platitudes are too easy for people to say. Get into deeper conversations than that. Really explore their thoughts and have a back and forth discussion.

8. How to talk to industry experts

The best people to talk to about your business ideas are industry and business experts, and potential customers. The problem is that business experts are also the most difficult to get a hold of. They are usually very busy.

But I'll give you a tip for how to easily get to talk to many industry experts. This won't work for some industries, but it will work for quite a few industries.

The tip is to join Facebook groups that are on the subject matter of your business niche or business idea or your overall industry. Usually there are large Facebook groups for just about any industry, and you can post questions there that many industry professionals will answer. You can try a similar approach with LinkedIn groups, but in the last few years Facebook groups have been taking over and becoming more popular than LinkedIn groups, so I would recommend exploring professional Facebook groups first.

Personally, I have gotten help from people in such groups on many different topics. Experts in such groups helped me grow my online courses, books, YouTube channel, mobile apps, podcast, and much more.

Lastly, you must talk to people who you think are potential customers. Identifying and reaching out to your potential customers depends on your industry and niche, and who those potential customers might be. Sitting here and writing, it is impossible for me to guess who your potential customers might be. Try to identify them and begin conversations with them ASAP. You don't have to start selling to them, but get their thoughts on your ideas and whether they would be interested in the kind of product or service that you are considering.

CHAPTER 8: PLANNING OF MONETIZATION STRATEGIES

"Great companies are built on great products."

- Elon Musk

1. Benefits of planning for long-term use and engagement

Earlier in this book I alluded to the tremendous benefits of having long-term clients, and now I want to focus on this more fully. Long-term clients are great for your business because they tend to buy more, recommend your business more, leave more positive reviews, and do other things that boost your business. But long-term clients don't just suddenly appear. They must be cultivated. And in a savvy business, that cultivation begins at the very planning stages of the business before the business even exists.

During the planning stages of your product or service, one of the things you must plan for is how to make your customers engage with your business long-term. Let me give you some examples to clarify this.

- When you buy a car, the car company want you to keep coming in for regular maintenance. When they build the car they also want to make sure that you love your car. Once you are comfortable coming back to the dealership for maintenance and you have a good experience with the car you bought from them, their goal is to sell you your next car and the car after that.

- In the example of my mobile apps, my goal is to make these apps long-term use apps that people use continuously throughout their experience of starting a business. If the apps become a daily tool for entrepreneurs, I win big because every time people open the app there is a chance that they might buy something new on it, leave a nice review, or do something else that would benefit me. Otherwise, if people discard the app after a short period of using it, I'll lose the opportunity to make money from them.

- Food companies make many kinds of flavors of their foods for a number of reasons. One reason is that you might want to try multiple flavors which for them means an immediate doubling or tripling of revenue. They also want you to love the food so you keep buying their products. If you buy some food long-term, the seller of that food will make 10,000%+ revenue from you as long as you keep on eating it over a period of months or years.

As small business owners we tend to obsess about getting new clients. But the ironic thing is that if our current clients love our product or service, it will be much easier to sell to existing clients than to find new ones.

With all this in mind, when you plan your company, try to plan for how you will position or create your product or service to make it a regularly consumed product or a product that becomes a part of people's daily life and habits. If you can accomplish that, you have a much stronger business case.

2. Long-term monetization strategies with their pros and cons

One of the most common long-term monetization strategies is the subscription model. The beauty of the subscription model is that a person can stay subscribed for many years and they have to do some work to unsubscribe. That creates an actual barrier for a person to stop being a customer which is amazing for you as a business owner.

Even when people stop using a product or service, they sometimes keep getting billed simply because they have not made the effort to unsubscribe. This often happens with gym memberships where people stop going to the gym, but they remain a paying member for months and sometimes years.

The problem with subscriptions is that people are afraid to sign up for them precisely because they know that there is a high chance of them stopping to use the service, but still paying because they might procrastinate on unsubscribing.

Luckily, there is a natural way for us to remove the hesitation in the mind of the consumers. That strategy is to sell consumable products. Consumable products are food, clothing, online credit, or points in a game or a mobile app, etc. You can even think of traditional services like lawn care as a consumable because people keep needing it over and over.

You have to structure your consumable products to make people really want them. The best way to do that is by making your product so good that people will want them again and again. Think about how well this works with food (or alcohol for some people). Once people like some food item, they keep buying it over and over. The other way to make people consume your products on a regular basis is by making people addicted to your product. For example, if you are playing a mobile app game and you can't beat a level, you might buy an in-app purchase for some extra lives to beat that level to get further in the game. But as soon as you get to the next level, the game gets even harder, and if you don't want the fun to stop, you keep buying lives and points to keep getting further in the game.

If you have a more traditional, non-tech service like a lawn care business, since grass keeps growing all the time, all you have to do is provide the service at a high enough level of quality and a reasonable price so that you get hired to provide the service on a regular basis. The same is true for many businesses like a barbershop, cleaning businesses, gyms, etc.

If your product isn't a natural fit the subscription or the consumable models, don't worry. There are many more ways to have a strong monetization strategy. The next strategy to think about is a slight reversal in how we have been thinking about monetization so far. While the subscription and consumable products strategies are predicated on a long-term relationship over which you make money, wouldn't it be great if you can just charge a significant amount of money upfront? That is available to you if you position yourself as a high-end brand.

If you are not a high-end brand, you can make more products cheaply. That opens up the possibility of taking advantage of the catalog revenue model where instead of selling one expensive product, you let people buy your products at significant discounts or simply cheap prices, but show them many products they can buy at once. Sometimes one person can snap up a bunch of products on a sale that together give you the profit of either one high-end sale, or the sum of a year worth of purchases in a subscription model. I personally like to use this model whenever I can because it leaves customers happy that they got great value, and I am happy that they spent money on a few products and not just one.

3. How to turn clients for any business into long-term clients

You may be planning to use social media to attract new customers as a part of your marketing strategy. But what if I told you that social media is equally effective at retaining existing customers?

If you get your customers to follow you on Twitter, like your page or group on Facebook, subscribe to your YouTube channel or podcast, connected on LinkedIn, or sign up for your updates in any other way, you can promote new offers, discounts, products or services to them as long as they are signed up for your updates. The more social media sites of yours the same person follows you on, the more likely they will see your promotions. The more promotions they will see, the more likely they will engage with that promotion. Of course, be careful not to over-promote. If they see enough promotions to get irritated and unfollow you, you will lose the ability to promote to them long-term.

Even past clients who wanted to buy from you again or potential clients who wanted to buy from you for the first time, but got distracted and forgot about your business because life got in the way, can get reminders about your business from your social media updates and re-engage with your business.

If you are able to engage your social media followers, your marketing can be just as effective as a subscription model since people will be buying from you on a regular basis. It can be even better because people would engage with your business on their own terms, without the friction of having to sign up to a monthly subscription.

At this point you might be wondering what is the most effective social network to get people to re-engage with your business. The answer is that email is the single most effective way to get people to re-engage with your business. Most online marketers put a great deal of importance on email and the ability it gives them to get into someone's inbox. If you create, grow and maintain a highly engaged email list, it can be a very powerful weapon for you to generate many more sales from your customers for months and years to come.

Whatever business you may be planning, do your best to plan for how to get client email addresses and to get them to follow you on social media.

CHAPTER 9: MAKING YOU A BETTER ENTREPRENEUR & STARTING YOUR BUSINESS

"Idease are easy. Implementation is hard."

- Guy Kawasaki

This chapter is a crash course on additional skills and knowledge you need in order to start a successful business. Each of the topics covered in this section is a broad topic in itself about which I could write a large separate book. In fact, there are many books covering each of the topics in this chapter.

What I'll do in this chapter is give a brief introduction to each of these topics to help you understand what kinds of topics might be good for you to research next.

If you are not quite sure what to do next for your business, I love hearing from people so feel welcome to send me your questions. The only thing I ask is that you please be brief in your questions because I get quite a bit of email, and I am often behind on answering it. Nonetheless, I'll be happy to hear from you. Also please mention that you are a reader of this book so that I understand how you got my email address. Here is my personal email address:

alex.genadinik@gmail.com

And hint-hint, if your email starts with something like "I read your business plan book, liked it, and left a nice review of it on Amazon" I will immediately appreciate you that much more, and will prioritize your email in appreciation.

And don't forget, many of the topics in this chapter are covered more fully in my online courses. You can get free access to one of my courses as a gift from me to you just for getting this book. At the end of this book is a full list of freebies that I made available for you. My full list of courses is listed there. Just browse the list of courses and tell me which complementary course you want. That can be a great way for you to keep learning without having to pay more for it.

1. Procrastination

People procrastinate for different reasons. For most people, the good news is that procrastination is a habit, and a habit is a learned behavior that can be reversed if you form a new healthier habit to replace the old habit which leads to procrastination.

Studies show that it takes about three weeks of daily behavior to form a new habit. You have to force yourself to do things in a new way, and after a few weeks you will no longer need to force yourself. The new healthier behavior will be your natural new behavior that you won't even have to think about.

The hardest parts of breaking your procrastination habit are taking the first steps to reverse your learned behavior and replacing it with another, and on a long-term basis not relapse to your old habits which caused you to procrastinate in the first place.

2. Motivation

There are two kinds of motivation: intrinsic and extrinsic.

Intrinsic motivation is something that comes from inside you. It is an inner drive you feel when you are excited about something, and doing what you love. This is usually a long-term motivation towards something that is just a part of you.

Extrinsic motivation is typically short-term motivation that you might get from an energetic song, treating yourself to a snack or a fun trip, or a motivational pep talk the effects of which dissipate minutes or hours before it is given.

While both types of motivation are great, you can guess that intrinsic motivation is going to be much more helpful to motivate you over the lifetime of your business

So how do you get this long-term intrinsic motivation? If you are working on the right things in life, and have put your life trajectory on a path that is the right one for you, much of your motivation will naturally be intrinsic motivation. On the other hand, if you've made some mistakes, gave into some life pressures, and are maybe not working on the things that excite you, then you will naturally be less motivated.

It all starts with getting to know yourself better and becoming more self aware to the point where you can understand what the right thing for YOU is to work on and pursue in life, and having the courage to pursue it. People who do that tend to be much more intrinsically motivated.

3. Focus, pomodoro, eliminate interruptions

Once you conquer your procrastination challenges and find the right kind of motivation and begin working, the next major issue people tend to face is how to get more done during the time they spend working.

There are many tactics and strategies to boost your work output, but arguably the single most effective way to dramatically improve your work output is to improve the quality of your focus. The more singular and prolonged your focus is on a given task, the more progress you will make while working on it, and your work will typically be higher quality work than if you had multitasked while working on the same task.

Your phone, Facebook, social media, extra open tabs on your browser, multitasking and people nearby, all decrease your productivity by distracting you and ruining your focus. The more you can reduce noise, alerts from friends, phones, websites, and other distractions, the more you will have a stronger focus on your task at hand, and immediately get more done.

Since it isn't easy to maintain laser focus for a long time, there is a very popular technique called the Pomodoro Technique where you choose a period of time during which you will have a singular and intense focus on one thing, followed by a scheduled break to refresh your mind and attend to distractions. For example, you can choose 30 minutes of work followed by 10 minutes of break, and repeat that cycle throughout the day. It doesn't have to be 30 and 10. You can choose the times that work better for your unique situation because you understand yourself better. If you are just starting out, you can even try as little as 10 or 15 minutes of intense focus followed by a short break.

4. Bigger picture focus for dramatic productivity boost

Whenever I see surveys of the top CEOs where they are asked about how they approach productivity, their answers are often that they do less by identifying less fruitful tasks and simply not doing those. For example, out of the ten things you have on your to-do list now, probably two or three of those will pay the highest dividends, and the others will be much less effective at getting you closer to your goals. The trick is to identify the tasks on your to-do list with the most potential and tasks with the least potential to get you closer to your most important goals. Once you identify the low-potential tasks, if they are time consuming, by taking them out of your to-do list you will immediately gain more time to work on the high-potential tasks and boost your productivity by focusing only on tasks that will get you closer to your goals.

5. Delegation/automation

Delegation, outsourcing and automation of processes are some of the tenants of productivity. As you work on your business, it would help you if you identify some of the inefficient areas or processes in your business, and consider whether they could be fixed by hiring outside help, finding free software to expedite some process, or even having some custom software built for you.

If you are just starting and you don't have a lot of money to spend on outsourcing or building of software, I would recommend to create a budget for yourself as low as $50 per month. That isn't a lot of money, but you would be surprised how many extra tasks you can get done if you outsource carefully and intelligently on websites like Fiverr.com or UpWork.com. Plus, this will give you practice outsourcing and automating more effectively for when your business grows and you have a bigger budget.

6. 3 types of business risk

There are three somewhat different types of risk you face when starting a business:

1) Product risk
2) Market risk
3) Financial risk

Not all businesses have each of these kinds of risk. As I explain what these are, think about which apply to your situation.

Product risk is the risk that your product may be too expensive, complicated, or difficult to produce, and may never get to market. Even if it does get to market, it will be too expensive to maintain and continue to improve. If you can't build or improve your product, you will never launch your business, and even if you do launch, it will be difficult for you to compete in the marketplace.

Some examples of such businesses are very high tech companies or ones with complicated software. What I often see is people hiring developers to create mobile apps. If you don't have software engineers as a part of your team, it will be more expensive to create your app or start-up product, and your product risk will increase.

The second type of risk is market risk. This is the danger that once you launch your product, customers won't buy it, and sales will be slow or nonexistent. Innovative products typically have more market risk where a cleaning or a lawn care business has nearly no market risk because these are such ubiquitous businesses that have a proven business model, it is well understood how to run them, and such services are widely in demand.

The third type of risk is financial risk. Some businesses have minimal financial risk and some have quite a bit. You have to know your situation and tolerance for risk, and make sure not to choose a business that is going to be more cash intensive than the amount of money you are prepared to risk.

7. Steve Blank and the Customer Development methodology

Steve Blank is a Stanford Business School professor, and a

3-time successful entrepreneur. His companies have either become billion dollar companies or have gone public in the stock market. He is one of the most respected business thinkers today.

He built his career on what he coined as the "Customer Development" methodology. The premise of this methodology is that instead of coming up with ideas of what customers would want and brainstorming these ideas with your team, you go "out of the building" and talk to your current and potential customers about their needs and what would help them most in your product or service. Talking to your customers takes any guessing out of the equation, and you can build a product that is ideal for your customers. Once your product is ideal for your customers, they will be much more likely to buy it, your business will grow, and you will find success.

Sounds simple, right? It isn't that simple, but today it is a widely used practice throughout the business world, and you should do it too in order to decrease your market risk.

8. Eric Ries and the Lean Start-up methodology

Eric Ries is Steve Blank's student and a very successful entrepreneur as well. Eric took Steve's Customer Development methodology to the next level with his Lean Start-up methodology.

The premise of the Lean Start-up is that instead of going to market with a fully built product, you go to market with a "minimum viable product" which is abbreviated as MVP. The advantage of the MVP is that it is fast, easy, and cheap to build. Having an MVP allows you to give it to your potential customers much faster. These customers will give you immediate feedback that you can then use to quickly improve the MVP and re-release it to give it to your customers again for another round of feedback that you can then use to again improve the MPV, making it better and better with every iteration of this cycle.

This creates a rapid feedback loop where you keep improving your product quality and innovation at a fast rate. The better you do this, the more you will stay ahead of your competition, and after enough such feedback loops your product will become the highest quality product in your market.

If you want to see an example of the Customer Methodology and the Lean Start-up methodology at work, look no further than this book. Throughout this book I encourage you to send me emails for different extra ways that I can help you. In the past when readers reached out to me, some of the conversations I had with them have informed me about how the book can be better, and those suggestions have gone into the next editions of this book. With every new edition of this book, I add more content that readers specifically asked for, making this book better for you and all the readers who will come next.

9. Reversing the no mentality

Many of the entrepreneurs I coach often say things like "if I only had money to start my business" or "I'll wait until I have more time in 3 months" or "I don't have an engineer to build my product so I won't start" or many other statements with a similar sentiment that the barrier they currently face will prevent them from starting their business.

Entrepreneurs find solutions to problems instead of letting

problems derail their businesses. If you find yourself not starting until some barrier goes away, try to change how you think about it. You must be resourceful and creative to find solutions to problems. Problems and barriers will always arise. They are just a part of the entrepreneur experience. Embrace them, and learn to solve them. Keep in mind that there are often many solutions to one problem, and you should try to discover all of them instead of sitting there despondent about how lack of something is preventing you from starting.

10. Your ego

As you start your business and especially if you manage to grow it, many people will praise you and tell you how smart and accomplished you are. Once you have any success, the praise only accelerates. As entrepreneurs we start to believe it.

Don't.

Always stay humble. Remember that while what you are doing is great, all of us still have much more to learn. My feeling is that this is a much healthier mindset. If you let your ego balloon and become too large, you will convince yourself that you don't need to improve anymore, and that will be the beginning of the end.

Instead, keep the attitude that you are always just at the relative beginning and you need to learn more and improve yourself in many ways as an entrepreneur. That will help your business much more.

11. Dealing with stress

Starting my business was one of the most stressful periods of my life. There is stress from lack of finances, business uncertainty, pressure from family and friends, self-doubt, etc.

If you are in the process of starting your business now, believe me, I understand what you are going through. Not only did I go through the same stressful period in my life, but I've coached many people who are in your exact situation.

Among the many negative things brought about by stress, one especially damaging byproduct of stress for your business is that it forces you to make short-term decisions aimed to make a quick buck instead of decisions that would benefit you long-term because you need to pay your rent and you are low on cash. I understand it. I was in that same boat before. But sometimes these short-term decisions and shortcuts make our long-term prospects worse.

For example, when I started my YouTube channel, I made many videos in the hope that they would get many views on YouTube and I would make money from ad views. But if I took the time to learn better video production and presentation, my earlier videos would have done much better long-term. Instead, most of my earlier videos are very low quality videos and get no views today. I didn't find growth for my YouTube channel until I stopped chasing the quick buck and took the time to learn how to make my videos better.

If you are familiar with the saying "haste makes waste," when you start your business, that haste is often forced by stress and the seeking of immediate benefits. It often creates a lot of waste. Be careful of the stress having too much influence over your business decisions.

12. Dealing with failure

Let's face it, as soon as you step out of your comfort zone, you will begin to fail. Try to see it as a good sign instead of a bad one. Every failure or criticism is either a sign that you are learning or a clue as to what you can improve. You can use those clues to unearth some of the blind spots in your business and fix them.

It is also much easier to accept failure or criticism if you don't let your ego become too big. When someone criticizes any of my products, it doesn't feel good, but deep down I know that their opinion can be shared by others, and if I listen to them closely, they can give me some amazing hints at what I can improve. Plus, we can even appreciate our critics for caring enough to take the time to voice their concerns.

In the spirit of this section, if you have some criticism of this book or have thoughts on how I can improve it, please send me an email with your suggestions and I'll appreciate your input. On the other hand, if you really like this book, by now you know that I would be grateful for a positive review of this book on Amazon.

13. Embracing work

I realize that business sounds exciting but in between all the glamour (is there really any glamour in it?) there is boring and unsexy hard work.

It's fun to plan, strategize, and dream about your business.

But none of those are the day to day things you do as you work on your business. The day to day is hard and often boring work. Many people hesitate at the prospect of hard work, but if you embrace it, you will give yourself a chance to be much more successful long-term.

14. Surround yourself with the right people

When you are starting your business, you should surround yourself with positive people who you can trust and who can give you additional good ideas for your business. This goes for business partners, co-workers, mentors or coaches, and even the friends you choose to surround yourself with.

You must work equally hard to get rid of people who bring negativity or distract you from your goal of working on your business. There are enough challenges in building a business and you must isolate yourself from any extra negativity or challenges that can be avoided.

15. Visualizing success

While it is important to do more than it is to dream about your business, dreaming about your success can be very helpful. Daydreaming about your success and visualizing success can help you see yourself after having met your business goals, and cement the reality of success in your mind.

Just like athletes visualize themselves hitting with winning shot, you have to visualize yourself being successful. That vision will draw you to itself almost as a magnet. Plus, it is fun to daydream.

The End

ADDITIONAL BOOKS TO HELP YOU PLAN, START AND SUCCEED WITH YOUR BUSINESS

1) Marketing Plan Template - this is the sister book for this book. Every business should have a strong business plan AND a strong marketing plan. A marketing plan is just a part of your overall business plan.

https://www.amazon.com/Marketing-Plan-Template-Example-marketing-ebook/dp/B0190HXUYG

Shortened URL if you are using a print copy of this book:

https://goo.gl/YU7sw6

2) 10 Fundraising Strategies - almost all entrepreneurs ask about raising money, and you may be wondering about it too. This book gives you 10+ different strategies to raise money for your business.

https://www.amazon.com/10-Fundraising-Ideas-Strategies-str ategies-ebook/dp/B00KADT0Q2

Shortened URL if you are using a print copy of this book:

https://goo.gl/3fqmBr

3) 20 Productivity Principles - this book will help you get more done regardless of what you are working on. I put together 20 different fields of productivity, each of which can give you the strategies to align your work in order to get more done starting today and every day for the rest of your life.

https://www.amazon.com/Principles-Productivity-Motivation-Or ganization-Procrastination-ebook/dp/B06X96T4FZ

Shortened URL if you are using a print copy of this book:

https://goo.gl/m6PZQ1

Here is a full list of my 20+ books on Amazon:

https://www.amazon.com/Alex-Genadinik/e/B00I114WEU

Shortened URL if you are using a print copy of this book:

https://goo.gl/WWBcao

Note: if you are in the UK, change the .com in the URLs to .co.uk

APPENDIX: FULL BUSINESS PLAN EXAMPLE FOR A MOBILE APP BUSINESS PLAN

NOTE: I used parts of this business plan in the chapter where we went through writing each section of a business plan. I added the business plan here at the end of the book so you can read it in one piece instead of jumping all over the place.

Title: Business plan for a business plan app

Executive summary

I am building a full 4-app mobile app series on Android and iPhone that will help people plan their businesses, and support them all the way through planning, starting and growing their businesses.

This is a revolutionary new take on mobile apps where the apps become the business coach and guides for entrepreneurs, and give them the support they need to succeed.

The reason there are 4 apps in the series is because each app covers one of the biggest challenges for entrepreneurs:

Business idea stage
Business planning stage
Fundraising guide

Marketing training

The full scope of the app coverage positions them to be the dominant mobile apps for entrepreneurs.

Product

These are mobile apps on Android and iOS. The apps help people create a business plan and aid them in starting a business.

The apps will help people with their businesses in these 4 ways. On each of the apps there are 4 main features that help entrepreneurs:

- Software tool to help people plan and save their plans right on the app. People will be able to create small business plans, fundraising plans and marketing plans on the app.

- Ability to plan parts of their business with business partners and invite their whole team to use the app with them (social sharing)

- Educational tutorials to teach the entrepreneurs about the business stage they are in: business ideas, business planning, marketing and raising money.

- Live help on the app provided by an expert. In most cases, until the app has sufficiently grown, to ensure quality of help, the coaching will be provided via text chat on the app by the founder, Alex Genadinik

Company Progress

- Founded in 2012
- 50-100% growth year over year in first 3 years
- 25% growth last year due to saturation on Android and lack of growth on iOS
- Next year focusing on iOS growth
- Over 1,000,000 cumulative downloads across all apps
- (Fictitious due to privacy) revenue last year: $125,000

Market research & target market

There is extensive research behind these apps. Until the apps reached 300,000 downloads, I (Alex Genadinik) answered every question asked on the apps. Not everyone asked a question, but many people did. Working with such a large sample set of entrepreneurs gave me an unprecedented view and understanding of the kinds of help they need, and the questions they have.

The idea for the app series is based directly on that market research of working with such a high volume of entrepreneurs on their businesses.

Besides business ideas, business planning, marketing and fundraising, entrepreneurs also asked about legal and accounting topics. I decided not to cover those topics directly within those apps. Instead, in the long-term the app will refer such clients out to correct law and accounting firms and professionals.

Demographics

- Largely under 35 years old (app users are usually younger)

- 35% US, 10% India, 5% UK, 5% Canada, 5% South

Africa, 4% Australia, 4% Malaysia, 3% Indonesia, 29% rest of the world including heavy leaning in the developing world since for many people there the smartphone is the only computing device they own.

- Low income

- Low education

- Not married

- No family

Psychographics

- Don't necessarily need to start a business, just need to make money one way or another

- Largely low tech businesses

- Typically not the Silicon Valley start-up types

- Under financial stress and pressure

- Low confidence in business, maybe told by others not to do business

- Little family support

- No ability to make in-app purchases with credit card due to being in the developing world. PayPal may be ok for some.

- Need a solution fast

- Have limited funds

- Prefer free

Competition

- Other business plan templating apps

- Gimmicky business plan apps that promise a business plan quickly by filling in the business plan sections with buzzwords

- Pen and paper planners

- Business card apps

- Business news apps

- Productivity apps

- Big budget apps

Marketing Plan

The marketing of these apps will be through

- Mobile app store search

- Publicity and PR (being a guest on the radio, podcasts and being mentioned by blogs)

- Social sharing from people inviting business partners to help plan the apps.

- My website http://www.problemio.com and Google

search where people find my website and apps that I promote there

- Google search

- My own YouTube channel where I promote the apps

- My own podcast where I promote the apps

- Ads on Facebook, Instagram, AdWords and YouTube AdWords

Since for most apps most of their downloads come from app store search, that is where I will concentrate.

Monetization (revenue streams)

- In-app purchases of content

- In-app subscriptions to coaching

- Up-selling coaching services off the app

- Up-selling my books and online courses

- Selling affiliate product like website hosting for new businesses and legal and accounting services

- Sponsors

NOTE: FICTITIOUS FIGURES (THE TRUE FINANCES OF THIS BUSINESS ARE PRIVATE)

Annual revenue: $125,000

In-app purchases of content $45,000
In-app subscriptions to coaching $30,000
Up-selling coaching services off the app $20,000
Up-selling my books and online courses $10,000
Selling affiliate product like website hosting
for new businesses and legal and accounting
Services $10,000
Sponsors $10,000

Next year projected revenue: $161,000

In-app purchases of content $60,000
In-app subscriptions to coaching $40,000
Up-selling coaching services off the app $25,000
Up-selling my books and online courses $12,000
Selling affiliate product like website hosting
for new businesses and legal and accounting
Services $12,000
Sponsors $12,000

Unit Economics (fictitious due to privacy with finances)

Since the product is a digital product and 99% of my
marketing is from free sources, there is no cost of goods or
marketing costs. Every download brings in (fictitious) $0.10 on
average LTV (lifetime value of a customer).

The LTV per customer is on par with other mobile app
businesses. Most apps struggle to make money per customer,
and make up for the lack of per customer revenue by
generating many downloads and having many customers.

Since this is a digital good, any revenue is pure profit.

Extending lifetime customer value (LTV)

- I use a "catalog" model to extent LTV by offering many upsells in the apps. I list all of my 20 books and 100+ online courses so when one person buys one, and they like it, they might buy a few more.

- I offer a subscription service on one of the apps. If a person subscribes for a year, that is 12 times more revenue than from a 1-time purchase, which represents a 1200% increase in revenue. And a 2-year subscription represents a 2400% increase in revenue from the same customer and so on.

- I offer long-term off-app business coaching which can generate thousands of dollars with the right client.

- Working on supporting the customers better and having them use the app longer with better design, more useful features, and more benefit to them. Longer engagement boosts monetization from those customers.

- Email collection and marketing

Profitability (Gross profit, net profit and operating profit)

Gross profit (income remaining after accounting of good sold) - in the fictitious finances of this business, that would be $123,000 annually since the only product creation cost is design.

Operating profit (subtracts additional costs of your business) - since in my business there are minimal other costs, after taxes on $12,000 (minus cost of design AND marketing AND accounting), I make $65,000.

Net profit - after I pay myself, $50,000 annually, the business profit is $15,000

Profit Margin:

Net profit / revenue: $15,000 / $125,000 = 0.12
$35,000 / $125,000 = 0.28
$65,000/ $125,000 = 0.52

Balance sheet (fictitious)

Assets:

Current assets:

Cash in the bank $50,000
Coaching clients payments owed to me: $3,000
Total: $53,000

Fixed assets:

Laptop: $1,000
Office supplies and furniture: $1,000
Trademark: $500
Total: $2,500

Liabilities: None

Outsourcing I owe: $500

Equity = $55,500 - $500
$55,000

Size of opportunity

The full potential for the apps is reached when they dominate search and recommendation algorithms on both Android and iOS.

Just with dominating search, these apps can reach about 1,000,000 people per year.

Once the apps are widely recognized by the app stores they can get big publicity and app store features that would result in 100,000-300,000 more downloads per year.

SWOT Analysis

Strengths: best in app store search, deepest customer understanding, personal care, years of experience improving product, ahead of competition

Weaknesses: limited resources to keep growing and experimenting

Opportunities: more app store domination and brand growth and awareness

Threats: easy barrier to entry. Bigger money apps can bump be off

Founding team

Single founder business.

Alex Genadinik: 5+ years software engineering, 10+ years marketing, 5+ years product creation, successful entrepreneur.

Previous funding and investor ownership:

None. Alex Genadinik retains 100% ownership

Costs

Under $2,000 per year in outsourcing design and feature
coding that I don't have time to code
Under $1,000 per year for marketing costs
After the apps are built, 5 hours of my time per month

FURTHER FREE RESOURCES TO HELP YOUR BUSINESS

Gift 1: I will give you one free online business/marketing course of YOUR choosing and huge discounts on any additional courses.

I teach over 100 premium, video-based online courses on business and marketing. I rarely give my courses out for free, but as a reader of this book, you get access to a course of your choice for absolutely free. Browse my full list of courses and email me telling me which course you want, and I will send you a free coupon!

Here is my full list of courses:

https://www.udemy.com/user/alexgenadinik/

Just send me an email to alex.genadinik@gmail.com and tell me that you got this book, and which one of my courses you would like for free. I will send you a coupon code to get that course for free.

Gift: 2: Get my Android and iPhone business apps for free.

My apps come as a 4-app course and on Android I have free versions of each!

Free Android business plan app:
https://play.google.com/store/apps/details?id=com.problemio&hl=en

Free Android marketing app:
https://play.google.com/store/apps/details?id=com.marketing&hl=en

Free Android app on fundraising and making money:

https://play.google.com/store/apps/details?id=make.money&hl=en

Free business idea Android app:
https://play.google.com/store/apps/details?id=business.ideas&hl=en

Free business idea iPhone app:
https://itunes.apple.com/us/app/small-business-ideas-help/id583498069?ls=1&mt=8

Free iPhone business plan app:
https://itunes.apple.com/us/app/business-plan-and-coach/id554845193

Free iPhone marketing app:
https://itunes.apple.com/us/app/marketing-advertising-articles/id587238156?ls=1&mt=8

Free iPhone app for fundraising:
https://itunes.apple.com/us/app/funding-fundraising-ideas/id624657810?ls=1&mt=8

Gift 3: Free business advice

If you have questions about your business plan or anything mentioned in this book, email me at alex.genadinik@gmail.com and I will be happy to help you. Just please keep two things in mind:

1) Remind me that you got this book and that you are not just a random person on the Internet.
2) Please make the questions clear and short. I love to help, but I am often overwhelmed with work, and always short on the time that I have available.

Gift 4: **More free products**

When I have free promotions for my products, the four places where I post them are my YouTube channel, my email list, Twitter, and my Facebook group. If you subscribe on all 4 or any of them, you will get my future updates about free products. Just keep in mind that I promote everything and anything business related on my social media accounts so it won't just be the freebies.

Here is my YouTube channel where you can subscribe:

http://www.youtube.com/user/Okudjavavich

Here is my Facebook group:

https://www.facebook.com/groups/problemio/

Here is a form where you can sign up for my email list:

http://glowingstart.com/email-subscribe/

You can also follow me on Twitter. I am @genadinik

COMPLETE LIST OF MY BOOKS

If you enjoyed this book, here is a shortened link for your convenience to check out my Amazon author page to see the full list of my books:
https://goo.gl/elbqem

DID YOU ENJOY THE BOOK?

If you liked the book, I would sincerely appreciate it if you left a review about your experience on Amazon.

And if you didn't enjoy it, or were expecting to get different things out of it, please email me at alex.genadinik@gmail.com and I will be happy to add/edit material in this book to make it better.

Thank you for reading and please keep in touch!

ABOUT THE AUTHOR

Alex Genadinik is a software engineer, entrepreneur, and a whiz marketer. Alex is a 3-time best selling Amazon author. His work has helped millions of people in the entrepreneurship space. You can learn more about Alex's current projects on his website:
http://www.problemio.com

Alex has a B.S in Computer Science from San Jose State University

Alex is also a prominent online teacher, and loves to help entrepreneurs achieve their dreams.

Here is a full list of books by Alex Genadinik on Amazon:
http://www.amazon.com/Alex-Genadinik/e/B00I114WEU

Here is a shortened URL for the full list of books:
https://goo.gl/uKk98y

Books recommended after this one:
Marketing plan template: https://goo.gl/YiCzCn

10 Fundraising Strategies: https://goo.gl/vgguq9

20 Productivity Principles: https://goo.gl/nQ5ZSX

Made in the USA
San Bernardino, CA
25 August 2017